WRITE WHAT YOU DON'T KNOW

10 Steps to Writing with Confidence, Energy, and Flow

Also available

Write What You Don't Know: Imaginative
Storm Writer Training (online course)

Also by James Navé and Allegra Huston

How to Read for an Audience:
and touch people's hearts

By Allegra Huston

Love Child: A Memoir of Family Lost and Found

A Stolen Summer (also published
as Say My Name; a novel)

How to Edit and Be Edited: and polish
your work to a professional shine

By James Navé

The Road

100 Days: Poems After Cancer

Write What You Don't Know

10 STEPS TO WRITING WITH CONFIDENCE, ENERGY, AND FLOW

Allegra Huston and James Navé

founders of the Imaginative Storm method

TWICE **5** MILES

TAOS – LONDON

ISBN 979-8-9867154-0-7 (paperback)
ISBN 979-8-9867154-1-4 (ebook)

Twice 5 Miles
P.O. Box 2999
Taos, NM 87571

twice5miles.com

Book design by Euan Monaghan
Cover design by Jason Anscomb

This book is set in FF Scala Sans, designed by Martin Majoor, with headers in Dolly Pro from the Underware type foundry.

Contents

Welcome to the Imaginative Storm

The idea for the Imaginative Storm comes from Charles Wright's poem "Lonesome Pine Special":

> What is it inside the imagination that keeps surprising us
> At odd moments
>   when something is given back
> We didn't know we had had
> In solitude, spontaneously, and with great joy?

What is it? You might call it your creativity or your creative soul. Or spirit, the Duende, the universe, or a higher power speaking through you. Perhaps it's not something "inside" the imagination—just your imagination itself, sparking.

It doesn't really matter what you call it. The important thing is to recognize that it's there in you, like it's there in every one of us. As humans, creativity is our birthright.

How do you invite your imagination to give you those gifts? That's what the Imaginative Storm method does: it gives you ways to energize your imagination, and trains your rational mind to catch them, value them, and shape them. As you work through this book, you'll learn how to bring about those joyful moments in your writing, and stretch them into a practice that you can call upon whenever you wish. Your imagination will gift you with unexpected juxtapositions, memorable turns of phrase, and passages that astonish you with their immediacy and depth of emotion. You might think to yourself, "I didn't know I had that in me!" But you do. You just have to find a way of letting it come out.

By the time you complete the ten sessions in this book, you'll have a portfolio of writing unlike anything you've written before—full of freshness and fizz, and absolutely true to your voice. Maybe you'll go on to develop some of these pieces into finished work, or maybe you'll just decide to cherry-pick the juiciest nuggets and drop them into a work-in-progress. Maybe you'll never open your Imaginative Storm notebook again, but your approach to writing, and your perspective on the world, will be transformed.

But how can you write what you don't know?

Have you ever had the feeling, as you were writing, that something "just came" to you? You didn't "think it up." It surprised you. Maybe it continued for long enough that you almost felt like you were taking dictation. You didn't know where your writing would go before it headed off somewhere, and all you had to do was follow it. When that happens, it's a delightful, energizing experience. You're curious about where that idea came from. It came so effortlessly! And you're hungry for more.

That "something" was a gift of your imagination. Fresh, original writing comes from the part of the brain that isn't your conscious, rational, intentional, hardworking mind.

When you write what you know, it's like you're looking straight ahead, your eyes focused down the path of some intention or agenda. When you write what you don't know, your focus isn't fixed straight ahead, and you can spot things out of the corners of your eyes. Those things are always there, but when you write with a fixed agenda, you never even see them.

When you tell a story you already know, you're recounting a

version that your rational mind has already organized and categorized and made meaning from. It's tidied away anything that didn't fit that version. There's a great deal of detail, observation, story, and emotion stashed away in your brain. The Imaginative Storm method gives you access to it.

"Write what you know" is one of those classic pieces of advice that only tells part of the story. Yes, if you're going to write about a plumber, it's a good idea to have some knowledge of plumbing. And if you're a stock trader, or an orphan, writing about stock trading or being an orphan is a good place to start. So when we say, "Write what you don't know," we're not saying, "Never write what you know." We're saying: Question what you know. Explore the edges of what you know. Trace the shapes of what's not present to your everyday, rational mind. Allow the unexpected room to emerge.

Writing with an "I don't know" mindset engages your curiosity. And if you're intrigued by where the writing is taking you, your reader will be intrigued too.

You might think of your memory, your everyday perceptions, and your view of yourself and the world as being like lace. The patterns of lace are made by what's not there as much as by what is there. The Imaginative Storm will shake up your memories, shake up the way you experience things, shake up your perceptions. What you know will still be there, but your focus will shift to what's beneath it. You'll explore the corners and shadows that the ordinary daylight of your thinking mind doesn't reach.

Why Write?

When you write, you deepen your conscious experience of life. You investigate your perspectives and judgments and motives. You become more attuned to what delights you and what depresses you. You appreciate a myriad of things that otherwise escape your notice. You explore the eternal question: why do we humans do what we do?

And when you write for a reader (or listener), you throw threads of connection across the distances between people. Your readers recognize themselves and their experience of the world when they read what you write. Their understanding of human nature expands. Their understanding of life's possibilities and the world around them expands. Your story is now part of their own.

Storytelling is one of the things that define us as human. We're all hardwired for story. We make sense of the world and our experience in it by tracing patterns in the things that happen. A story takes a snippet of life and gives it shape and meaning. That story could be as pointed as a blog post or as wide-ranging as *War and Peace*, as factual as a news article or as fanciful as *Alice's Adventures in Wonderland*.

Shaping your perceptions into words gives form and meaning to your experience of living. You refine your ideas. You imbue people and events with importance and purpose. You explore your own emotional spectrum—and other people's. A surge, which can be as warm as a bath or as sharp as a cattle prod, stirs your creative spirit. The muse, or the Duende, or the dragonfly of inspiration, beckons you to follow it.

But then, often, you hit a wall. The words on the page aren't the words you heard in your head. What you write feels secondhand, tired, overworked, unsatisfying. It's hard labor, heavy lifting. Maybe you think, "I can't do this!"

You can. We all can. But many of us have let our imaginations go weak from lack of use, just as we might have let the strength of our muscles fade away. That's why we call our course Imaginative Storm Writer Training—because it restores the strength and suppleness of your imagination.

What Is Writer Training?

Think of it like this: if you're going to run a race, you don't just get up off the couch and start running. You train. You get your muscles and lungs strong and your confidence up. You stretch your body and get a sense of its potential.

Or let's say you're a pianist preparing to play Carnegie Hall. You run scales, you practice trills, you try out different ways of pedaling. You don't just turn up and launch into Beethoven.

Like your body or your musical talent, your creative mind becomes more powerful when you train. When you stretch your imagination, it gets more supple. When you challenge it, it gains strength. Pretty soon, it gets sassy and wants to surprise you with its new range of abilities. Imaginative training works because we are all naturally creative creatures.

But because we all think in language and we know how to put words on the page, it seems like writing should be different from running a race or playing an instrument. So most of us assume that we should automatically be able to write in a way that satisfies us, straight out of the gate. Maybe you've thought, or heard someone say, "Why can't I write what's in my head!" In fact, the thoughts in your head are only partly in words, and most of them churn away beneath your conscious attention. It's not like turning on a tap and water comes out.

Question that assumption! You may, in the past, have judged your writing stiff and self-conscious, or flat and dull, and decided that you're just not a good writer. We're here to tell you that that isn't the case. You've just been expecting something unrealistic. Nobody told you what most professional writers have learned: that "good writing" is very rarely born that way.

We call our process "writing from the Imaginative Storm to the creative form." The important part of this is that the creative form comes later. If, up to this point, you've been unsatisfied by what you write, that's probably because you've been starting too close to the finish line.

"Generating material" vs. "writing"

At this stage, it can be helpful not to call the process of putting words on a page "writing" at all. We prefer to call it "generating material." Why? Because when you're not "writing," you don't feel that you're supposed to write well.

Most of us grew up with the idea that we have to "get it right." That it's up to us to expend effort to make something turn out how we want it. Therefore, when you write without understanding that you need to train first, you try to write well.

We believe that *trying* to write well is one of the biggest obstacles to writing well.

"But," you may say, "I don't naturally write well, so I have to try!" If you've been suffering from writer's block, or writer's frustration, this may be the reason why. Trying doesn't help you. It's not will and effort that you're lacking. What you're lacking is the right kind of inspiration, and the right target for the stage you're at. So please, let go of that "get it right" paradigm and replace it with this one:

Mess is currency, not a liability.

When you have currency, you're rich. Mess is where the surprises come from. When you're "generating material" rather than "writing," you can appreciate the value of mess—and when you do that, you signify to your imagination to amplify its activity. So, once you stop trying to produce good writing, you can generate really good material.

Freeing yourself from having to get it right allows you to respond to your own internal rhythms—which echo nature's messy rhythms. Is there such a thing as "getting it right" in nature, as opposed to getting it wrong? Is one arrangement of atoms better than the rest?

A cornerstone of Imaginative Storm Writer Training is to not be attached to whether anything you write will be usable or not. If this seems like a waste of time, reconsider that thought. Does a surfer feel that the hard work of paddling out beyond the break and the time spent waiting for the right wave are wasted? Does a serious skier think time in the gym is wasted? The creative improvisation of the Imaginative Storm serves the same purpose. It's what will make your "serious" writing original, zesty, and memorable.

You can always add polish later. You can't add surprise.

The dance between your rational mind and your imaginative mind

Maybe, in the past, you've been urged by a writing teacher to "get out of your rational mind." Is that even possible? You're a rational creature. You can't just switch off your rational mind, or kick it off like shoes.

If you've ever tried to make your rational mind shut up for more than a few moments, you probably felt like you were failing. Maybe you thought it was your lack of talent. Or some psychological problem holding you back. Once again, it's not your fault. That's just another paradigm that needs to be reset.

So, don't fight a losing battle. Honor your rational mind! It has gifts to give you, too. For now, just ask it to give up control. We call it letting your rational mind dance with your imaginative mind. It takes two to tango, as we all know—but one partner leads, the other follows. As you write in these 10-minute bursts, let your imagination take the lead. Let your rational mind follow it wherever it goes.

The stormy material you'll generate during the Writer Training is not even close to being finished work. You may use some of it in your finished work, next week or decades from now—but you can't know that as you write it. You can use the writing prompts in this book to expand your thinking around a project you're working on, but we urge you not to try and write something that with a bit of editing will end up in the final draft. When you impose an agenda on your Imaginative Storm writing beyond mere exploration, your imagination seizes up. It doesn't like being told what to do. Writing words that you hope will be usable in more or less the order you're putting them in puts your rational mind back in the driver's seat. Instead of dancing, you'll be trying to go somewhere, and the wrong member of the team is in the lead.

At first, you may find it difficult to cede rational control of what you're writing to the whims of your imagination. But the more you let go, the more you will enjoy letting your imagination twirl and whirl and swirl you into nonsense and unreason and questions and blazing new insights—and back again.

You'll feel this sense of fun and flow in your body. The tension and tightness caused by trying to write well disappear. Your mouth, which may have tightened into a fierce line or yearned for a cookie, might even be smiling.

How to Use This Book

Imaginative Storm Writer Training is made up of 10 sessions plus a finale to send you into your writing future. In the course of these 10 sessions, you will:

- Train your rational mind to dance with your imagination— and let your imagination lead the dance
- Discover and develop your own voice
- Bring freshness and emotional depth to your writing
- Train your inner critic to be helpful rather than harmful
- Teach your intuition to recognize the elements of a strong, compelling story
- Sharpen your awareness of the world around you
- Develop new insights and perspectives on yourself, your life, and other people

You'll need about 90 minutes to complete each session. You can do the entire Training in 10 days or less, or stretch it out over 10 weeks or more. Whatever your schedule, make a commitment to yourself to show up on a regular basis.

Between the sessions, we've placed short discussions on the core principles of the Imaginative Storm. Each discussion relates most specifically to the session that precedes it, but they can be read in whatever order works best for you. You might like to read them all before you start the Training, or save them for last.

When we do the Writer Training in a workshop setting, everybody reads out what they wrote after each prompt. So, you may wonder why we don't include samples of writing exercises here. Answer: because you might be tempted to read them before you write to the prompt yourself, and that will undercut the power of the Imaginative Storm for you. You might think you're supposed to do the prompt a certain way because of the pieces we chose to include. And you're not! There's no "right" way to do any of our prompts. Interpret each prompt according to the direction your own imagination and life experience sends you in. That's the way you should do it—however *you* do it. The way your imagination storms is not the way anyone else's imagination storms.

You'll find examples of 10-minute writing to many different prompts on the Imaginative Storm Circle site: follow the link at imaginativestorm.com. Please post your own Writer Training pieces under the space "10-Minute Triumphs," so we (and other writers) can read them!

What tools will you need for this course?

Three things:

- [ ] a pen
- [ ] paper
- [ ] a timer of some kind, probably your phone

Longhand vs. computer

Write by hand if you possibly can. First, because it unplugs you from the digital space. Second, because there's some kind of hot-wire that happens between the imagination and the page. Maybe it's because we all learned to write by hand before we learned to type, or because when we drew, as children, we made an association between creativity and the hand moving across paper. Also, there are pressure points on the side of the hand that connect to the heart.

The pen is like a magic wand, inviting your body to relax and let buried memories and insights come out. When you write by hand, it connects you to the emotional tones in your body. The pen becomes an extension of your hand, and it urges you to keep moving. It's a different rhythm than typing on a keyboard. You'll start to notice that your pen reflects your mood: when you're upbeat, you'll write faster; when you're more contemplative, you'll write slower. You just feel more connected to the words.

You might say, "But I type so much faster than I write. I won't be able to keep up with my thoughts!" Well, lucky you. You'll just write messier. And if you can't read what you wrote, remember: mess is currency, not a liability. Now you won't be so tempted to go back and read over what you wrote, and start tinkering with it and judging it. Your rational mind will find it harder to take control of the dance and pull you out of the flow.

Writing on a computer has a finished look to it, and that invites your inner critic to butt in. It's super easy to read, and super easy to change things, and before you know it you're in editing mind or, worse, self-judging mind. You may be saying, "This is garbage" and "I can't write at all—what do I think I'm doing?" And if that mental dialogue sounds familiar, you know what comes next: you give up.

When you write by hand, it looks like a rough draft. It doesn't look like it's supposed to be good, or grammatical, or anything at all. You can still go back and cross out or add a word or two in order to set something up, but soon it gets hard to read so the dynamic makes you want to move on, rather than keep messing around with your words.

Also, you deal with emails on your computer, you write business letters on your computer. When you sit at your computer, you're likely to be in a "getting it done" frame of mind. Anything you can do to free yourself from the expectation of having to write well or having to accomplish a task will help you.

You may want to type up what you wrote later, with the thought that you might use some or all of it in a finished piece. So it seems like extra effort to write by hand, then type it up. Trust us on this one. The results will convince you that the extra effort is worth it.

If writing by hand is absolutely impossible for you, there is one further option: dictate into a transcription app. It doesn't work for everybody, but it might work brilliantly for you. Give it a shot.

Pen

If you already have a pen that you really like using, great. If not, treat yourself to a shopping expedition and test-drive a few different types. Ballpoints can be scratchy, so try a rollerball. A good pen flows easily across the paper, so that you don't actually feel your hand physically making the marks. It's easy to hold, not too fat, not too thin—you shouldn't get writer's cramp in just 10 minutes. If you want to splurge on a gorgeous fountain pen, go ahead—but only if it doesn't make you feel like you're supposed to produce "good writing" with it.

Try out different colors and notice how they make you feel. This may not be something you've paid attention to before. Black can feel somber or overly important. Green or purple might give you freedom to write something wild and crazy—or might make you feel that you're *supposed* to write something wild and crazy, which isn't helpful. We want to take all of the "supposed-to"s out of this. If you notice any other "supposed-to"s along the way that are particular to you, do what you can to remove them.

Always have a spare pen handy in case the first one runs out of ink.

Paper

A beautiful notebook might make you worry that you'll ruin it by writing badly in it. You don't want to have to live up to your notebook.

One of our participants writes in a nicely bound journal of blank pages but goes backward through it. Others use cheap and cheerful school notebooks or even loose sheets of printer paper. Sometimes even ruled lines and spiral binding feel demanding!

If you're using a notebook, dedicate it to your Imaginative Storm

Writer Training. It's a gift to yourself to take your activity seriously. If you're using loose sheets of paper, keep them in a folder—again, take your writing seriously even if it's "throwaway" (more on that later). And if, further down the line, you want to use something you wrote in the Training, you'll be able to find it.

Now, where are you going to sit?

If your desk makes you feel that you're supposed to write well, sit somewhere else. Curl up in an armchair. Prop yourself up in bed. Check out a lap desk, which is basically a cushion with a little wooden desktop glued to it. Or just use a large-format hardback book as a writing surface.

If you can, choose a time when nobody else is home—that way you won't feel self-conscious. You might even find a spot away from home: a friend's house while they're at work, a bookstore with comfortable chairs, a coffee shop with quiet nooks, the library. Do all the sessions in the same place if at all possible. That's part of the message you're sending to yourself: that in this practice, you're showing up for yourself. Even when you're generating mess, you're taking yourself seriously.

Session 1:
Spin the Kaleidoscope of Your Mind

The first thing you'll do in the Writer Training is free yourself from the expectation of writing well—or even making rational sense. We've already talked about how trying to write well is a major obstacle to writing well. So the plan here is to kick this whole idea firmly out of the way.

When you spin the kaleidoscope of your mind, you'll produce writing that's unlike anything you've ever written before. It will be fantastical, giddy, and it probably won't make much sense. Does that make you say, "Wait a minute! I don't want to waste my time! I'm a serious writer!" If so, great. But just because you take yourself seriously as a writer doesn't mean you can't play—especially when playing is the way that humans (and many other animals) learn.

We want you to get comfortable with the idea that much of what you write while you're training won't seem to be directly relevant to your "serious" writing. Pianists run scales, guitarists noodle around with chords. Those scaly flights and noodlings will never be recorded for public consumption or played for an audience. But are they helpful, even essential? You bet. In the same way, playing with kaleidoscope prompts expands the range and power of *all* your writing.

In twenty years of teaching writing workshops, we've seen the immediate and lasting benefits of kaleidoscope writing. Here's why:

- It teaches your rational mind to stop expecting "good" every time you put pen to paper.
- It encourages you to write what you don't know.
- It invites your imagination to surprise you.
- It teaches your critical mind to value that surprise.
- It encourages you to just enjoy words for the fun they can provide.

Dropping the stakes way below the point of publishability sends a clear and dramatic message to your imagination: GO BIG! Bring it! And it sends an equally clear message to your rational mind: logic and judgment aren't needed while the words are landing on the page. What's needed are openness and trust.

We're asking you to trust our method—because we know it works—but what we're really asking you to do is to trust your own creativity.

Heads-up: this session, on the page, is much longer than the others. In practice, it isn't. Since this is your first experience of the Imaginative Storm method, in Session 1 we explain our process step by step.

Prompt: A provocative image

You'll start spinning the kaleidoscope of your mind by coming up with a provocative image. This absurd, impossible image will be catnip for your imagination.

The important thing is to make absolutely sure your provocative image *does not* make rational sense. Here's an example: a zebra on a trapeze eating a pineapple. That doesn't make rational sense, but your imagination can't help but picture it. On the other hand, a zebra on the savanna eating grass makes rational sense, but does it excite your imagination?

Step 1: List ten things

The first step in building your provocative image is to list ten random things. Here's a sample list: *pothole, toolbox, pumpkin seed, accordion, giant squid, Mount Everest, spatula, big toe, mechanical bull.*

Now it's your turn. Generate your own list of ten random things.

Step 2: Build a provocative image

Choose a thing from the list you just made—something that brings a smile to your face. Next, locate it somewhere and give it something to do. Here's the formula:

Thing + Location + Action = Provocative Image

Make the location and the action as illogical as possible. For example:

- *A spatula dances around the Empire State Building wearing a frying pan*
- *Mount Everest reclining in satin sheets swats flies*
- *An accordion rides a mechanical bull while picking its toenails*

Give it a try. Build three provocative images, using three things from your list.

You now have three provocative images. Your rational mind looks at them straight on and says, "This is ridiculous." But your imaginative mind looks at them sideways and thinks, "This could be fun!"

Don't worry—it's only for a few minutes. Your imaginative mind is not going to break things and trash the house. Let it off the leash of reason, and who knows? Your rational mind may even enjoy not having to do all the work. It might still try to complain and criticize, but that's fine. You're training it.

And when you read over what you wrote, your rational mind will appreciate the new energy in your writing.

Step 3: Generate stormy words

You'll want to do this on a loose sheet of paper, or one you can rip out of your notebook.

First, choose one of your provocative images. Then, say it out loud. Believe it! Give it all you've got. Why? Because that's what starts the kaleidoscope of your mind spinning.

The moment you finish saying your provocative image out loud, put pen to paper and start generating a list of random words.

What's the first word that pops into your mind? Write it down. Then the next, and the next. See if you can generate 60 words in 2 minutes.

Don't question the words as they come. They don't have to have anything to do with the provocative image. They don't have to have anything to do with one another. If your imagination veers away from your starting point, great. If it falls in love with the provocative image and sticks close, great. If a short phrase pops into your head, jot it down.

Write fast. If you're stuck for a word, just write "blah blah" or write the previous word again. Keep this as a list, not joined-up writing.

Ready? Say your provocative image out loud now. With gusto! Then . . .

Set your timer (2) **and generate words**

How many words did you get? (You don't have to count them.) Most people get 25–30. If you got 60, congratulations.

Step 4: Improv your stormy words

Read your words aloud. Notice that as you do, some of them start to join up. For example, here's a list of words prompted by one of the sample phrases above:

no-way	*force*	*bingo*
bold	*backstop*	*creature*
becoming	*jump*	*string*
boom	*NYC*	*line*
bless	*believe*	*bars*
begin	*doubt*	*wishes*
run	*bong*	

You can read across the columns as well as up and down, or jump around:

> *no-way, becoming bold boom*
> *NYC, believe doubt*
> *jump bingo wishes*
> *backstop bong*

Take some time to play around in your list. Say the words aloud—it matters. Your imagination likes it. It gets jazzed up by the weird kinds of sense that start emerging.

Enjoy the rhyme and rhythm, the babble of meaning, the myriad colors of these kaleidoscopic words.

Are you smiling yet?

You can play favorites; you don't have to be fair and use all the words equally. Let your rational mind join in, by adding extra words to build phrases that just might make some mini-smidgin of sense, for example:

Force that no-way bong string
Believe bong wishes
Bless bong doubt
Make doubt a no-way one-way run

Now, build some longer phrases with your own list of words.

We hope you're having fun—but maybe you aren't. Maybe your rational mind doesn't want you to play, because it thinks playing is not appropriate for a serious writer. Or because it doesn't want you to look ridiculous, even to yourself. That's just your inner critic trying to keep you safe. It reckons that if you feel dumb or dim or self-conscious, you'll stop. Remind yourself that even if this feels ridiculous now, it's going to benefit you in the long run. Reassure your rational mind that playfulness and seriousness are not contradictory.

We've talked about letting the rational mind dance with the imaginative mind, and letting the imaginative mind lead the dance. When you write to a kaleidoscope prompt, it can be like a tango in triple time. With practice, you'll find your rational mind laughing and gasping for breath as your imagination spins it around in dizzying circles and flying dips.

Step 5: Put it on paper

The only difference now is that your delivery system is pen and paper, rather than your voice. Your prep work has stirred up your imagination, and you've felt those little bursts of energy that surprising combinations of words give you. Keep the same looseness as you generate material on the page.

Here's what you'll do:

Put your list of words in front of you, and let your eyes roam across the words until one of them hooks your imagination. Start there and follow wherever your imagination takes you.

You can keep glancing at your list of words for more inspiration, or just go off in some direction and never return to the word list at all. Don't worry about making what you write coherent. Don't try to create a logical through-line if one isn't appearing on its own.

Remember: mess is currency. Mess is your goal here.

Set your timer  **and write now**

Before you read what you wrote aloud, let's assess:

- Did you feel any tension between what you thought you'd write, or what you thought you were supposed to write, and what you were actually writing?
- Did you feel unsure about where your writing was going?
- Did you think, "This is ridiculous," and kept writing anyway?

If you answered yes to any of those questions, great! That's the feeling of your creative muscles stretching.

When you're working in the Imaginative Storm, you will often have no idea what comes next. You'll surprise yourself with what you put on the page. The more you let your imagination go wherever it wants to go, the more energized your writing experience will be— and the sparkier the raw material that you generate, which you can revise into polished pieces later.

Step 6: Read what you wrote aloud

You might be thinking, "Do I have to? That was a load of codswallop!"

Answer: yes. Here's why.

Hearing what you wrote, and animating it with the warmth and energy of your breath, is a totally different experience from letting the words just sit on the page. Reading aloud has two seemingly contradictory advantages: it gives you a degree of objectivity, and it also brings you closer to what you wrote. You start to feel a sort of tenderness for it, like you do for your young child's artwork.

When you read silently, you're more critical. You notice what you think is feeble more than what has energy. But when you read aloud, you actually feel the sparks—little pops of excitement in your body when some combination of words surprises you. Maybe a musical rhythm, a striking juxtaposition, a detail of description or emotion that feels bright and sharp.

Some of what you hear will surprise you—it didn't feel quite like that when you were writing it. You'll notice nuances that you'd miss if you only read your work over silently. You'll start to find your own mind intriguing.

Read aloud now

How was that for you?

Perhaps you've read your work aloud before. Even so, have you ever read something that raw aloud? Was the experience different? In what ways?

If you've never read your work aloud before now, the sound of your voice may have surprised you. Even if you found you didn't actually like it much, soon you'll fall in love with the way your voice sounds as it makes an imprint on the air with the words you put together using your skills and your imagination.

From now on, read everything you write aloud. Read it with curiosity about what you have to say. Don't be tentative, even if you think it's not "good": allow yourself to appreciate even the tiniest moments of energy. This is just material; it's not supposed to be "good." Which doesn't mean it isn't good—but you can decide what's good and what isn't later.

Adding emotional depth

Emotion is the life force flowing through the veins of your writing. Moods and hopes and fears determine and color every human action. Whatever activity you're engaged in, however dry it is, your emotions are engaged too—and other emotions are swirling beneath the surface.

The presence of emotion in your writing is what makes your reader's mirror neurons fire. In other words, when a reader recognizes something they've felt themselves, they feel it again—this time, along with the character you put on the page. And, as well as engaging your reader, emotion engages you, the writer. When you care about what you're writing, you have the motivation and energy to keep pressing ahead, even when things aren't flowing as freely as you wish they were.

You almost certainly know that writing something like "I was happy" doesn't convey nearly as much as the feeling of a warm spring sun on your skin, or breaking into a dance as you walk down the street, or snuggling in bed with a purring cat. Could you write any of those scenes without feeling happiness as you describe them?

Well, you could, if you're just writing what you know—replaying a moment as if you'd recorded it on video. But when you move away from that recorded memory, into what you don't know at the moment of writing, you take yourself back into the scene and feel the emotion once again. Emotion doesn't cross the space between writer and reader if it's just described from the outside. You have to feel it inside, as you write.

Few emotions are plain and straightforward; they come in different shades. The sun on your skin might be more like pleasure, the dance might be more like delight, the snuggle with your cat more like contentment. But you don't need to label your emotions—to yourself or on the page. The goal is to evoke emotion in your reader by conveying the sensations of an experience, not tell them what to feel with abstract words. The distinction we just made is simply a way to encourage you to zero in on the specifics of how you feel. The more nuanced the emotion you feel as you write, the more detailed and powerful your writing will be.

Prompt: Other people's words

This time, instead of spinning the kaleidoscope of your mind, you'll borrow words from other writers.

You may be thinking, "Wait a minute! I thought you told me not to write like other writers." That's correct. You're not going to write like other writers. You're going to write like you—and feel the difference.

You may also be thinking, "But that's plagiarism." It isn't. Plagiarism is taking another person's work and presenting it as yours. What you'll be doing here is taking inspiration from other writers' work and creating something of your own. Many excellent poems were written "after" a poem by someone else.

Words are our common resource: they belong to everyone who knows them. Nobody owns a word (though corporations like to trademark them). Combinations of words may "belong" to a particular writer, but you can give them new dimensions and even new meanings. Let's say you write, "Out, damned spot!" It's plagiarism if your character is sleepwalking, haunted by a murder they provoked. But it's a perfectly allowable allusion to *Macbeth* if your character is cleaning the rug where their brother dropped a quesadilla while watching the Super Bowl.

Still, let's say you slip up and what you write is close to plagiarism. So what! Artists go to museums and copy famous paintings all the time. This is training. You can do whatever you want.

Here's what you'll do in this prompt:

First, find two poems to fish from. Go to imaginativestorm.com/listen-to-poems and choose two that you don't know well. Even though all the poems we've recorded come from past centuries (and are out of copyright), the words that fall out of those poems onto your list will have their own present-day vibe—and so will the piece you write.

As you listen to the poems, fish words from them, and write the words on another loose sheet of paper. Let the words flow past you without worrying about the meaning of the poems. If you feel like you don't have enough words, pick a third poem and add some more.

Once you're done fishing:

Create a separate list of emotion words. Here are some to get you started:

ecstatic	determined	paranoid
sad	serene	bored
afraid	worried	obsessed
miserable	terrified	satisfied
joyful	grieving	exasperated
disgusted	contemptuous	appalled
anxious	frustrated	walking on eggshells

Write down the ones that grab you on another loose sheet of paper. And add a dozen more of your own.

Now, look over your list of emotion words until your imagination lands on an emotion that you can bring up in yourself right now. Let it take you back to a time when you felt that emotion strongly. Feel it again as intensely as you can.

You may notice that other emotions become part of the mix. You've probably felt angry at someone you love, or been both excited and anxious at the start of a journey, or felt some mixture of fear and guilt and determination and righteousness just before you confess an uncomfortable truth.

Keep feeling that emotion as you turn to the list of words you fished from the poems. Let your eyes roam over them until one word hooks into the emotion you're feeling. Start there.

Write anything you want. Use as many or as few words from the list as you like. The important thing is to stay in your emotional state and keep the dial turned high.

Set your timer (1 0) **and write now**

When you're finished, read what you wrote aloud.

Recognizing your voice

Working with borrowed words is excellent training for recognizing your voice in your writing. You've just written a piece using words that, when you heard them, were in somebody else's voice. When you read your piece aloud, you probably felt some moments when the borrowed words became your own, and other moments when they felt like they were still in somebody else's voice.

Read your piece aloud a second time, paying closer attention to your own response in the moment. Do you notice any difference between passages that felt like your voice, and passages that didn't feel like your voice? Reading your work aloud develops your authenticity meter: with practice, you'll be able to feel in your body when you're on your voice and when you're not.

As you get comfortable with reading your raw material aloud, you'll realize that you've found your voice. If, like so many "aspiring" writers, you've felt stressed by the need to find your voice, you might think, "Can it really be that easy?" Yes, it can. Why? Because, surprise, surprise, your voice has been there all along. You just had to get out of the way and let it start making patterns on the air.

So, why would anyone ever think they need to find their voice?

We'd say it's because they've been trying to write well. When you're trying to write well, you're trying to write like writing that you think is written well—which, by definition, was written by somebody else. (That "somebody else" could even have been you, a few years ago.) So, no wonder it doesn't sound like you!

Here's the secret: stop trying to write well, and your voice will be right there.

That may take a bit of practice, because of course you want to write well. So do we. But you want to write well as *you*, not trying to sound like somebody else. *You* have to be in there from the start.

Times will come during the Writer Training when you don't know what to write. Possibly you'll fall back into an old pattern of "trying," instead of simply waiting for something to come. If that happens, be glad! You have an opportunity to glean good information. Notice how you tense up. Notice how you lose touch with the experience you're writing about. Notice how your focus contracts to the confines of your skull, and you lose touch with your bodily senses. Notice how, when you read the piece aloud, your voice feels constricted or goes higher or starts to sound artificial.

And then, hopefully, if you let your imagination take the lead, you'll find yourself back on your voice. You'll feel a rush. Maybe you even feel a bit giddy. The words flow. Okay, they're not a finished draft, but what they have in them is *you*.

Prompt: "I don't remember"

For the last prompt of this session, you're going to write about what you don't remember. That may sound weird, even impossible. But as we've discussed, one of the cornerstones of the Imaginative Storm method is writing what you don't know rather than what you know.

So here goes:

Think of an event or a place or a person you know very well. Something that's important to you. Focus on it, visualize it, bring it up as fully as you can in your imagination. Feel the emotions associated with the memory.

Now, begin writing with the words: "I don't remember . . ."

We're not asking you to invent details you've actually forgotten. Remember the image of lace: the pattern is made by what's not there. What we're asking you to do is to trace those negative spaces in your memory.

You may find, as you write, that you remember things you thought you'd forgotten—but don't let that draw you back into what's familiar about the memory. Keep your focus on what you don't remember.

Set your timer (10) **and write now**

When you're finished, read what you wrote aloud.

Starting with "I don't remember" gets you out of your official version of a memory, the way you've always told it. That's why you may remember details you thought you'd "forgotten"—your rational mind stashed them away because they didn't support the interpretation of events it had created.

If you've tried to write up this memory before, likely it was your "official version" that you recounted. Probably it felt rather flat, only half-alive, but you couldn't figure out why. Notice how this version is so much more immediate and emotional and authentic. The negative space in a memory adds a sense of mystery, of unknowns, of other possibilities—which is the experience of actual living, rather than remembering. Acknowledging the gaps makes your writing feel immediate and honest. After all, nobody remembers everything.

When you take the Imaginative Storm approach, you can poke around in the memory, turn it to different angles, question it, maybe find an entirely new meaning in it. "I don't remember" is an invitation to your body to pull up what your consciousness has forgotten.

One of the most dramatic instances of this was a psychotherapist in one of our workshops who was convinced she'd had the perfect happy childhood. In fact, she mentioned it so often we got suspicious. Then, when she wrote about her parents borrowing her savings when she was ten years old and how guilty she felt about wanting to be paid back (which didn't happen), she suddenly saw that this was not an episode from a perfect happy childhood! Her story of her life changed in a flash—and some previously unresolvable contradictions started to resolve for her.

Over the years, we've listened to hundreds of people read what they wrote to this prompt. Often they begin with something like "I don't remember what the weather was" or "I don't remember whether her eyes were blue or gray," and immediately, everyone listening is drawn in. The negative space in a memory is magnetic, maybe because it suggests that the event you're about to recount is so intense that, like a blinding light, it has wiped the details away.

Instead of the hard, polished surface of certainty, "I don't remember" acknowledges the porousness of memory. And it allows your reader to enter, bringing in memories of their own.

Using "I don't remember" for writing memoir and fiction

If you're writing a memoir, you might think you're supposed to remember everything, and if you don't, you should interview people and do research to discover as much as possible about what actually happened. But unless you're writing about incidents of historical importance, that's actually not necessary. You're not taking an exam on your life or presenting evidence in court.

Your story is not the record of events that happened to you. Your story is the way in which you met them and responded to them—how you influenced them, and how they changed you. Your emotional journey is the story, not the circumstances whose details you may or may not remember.

Just because you're writing a memoir, you're not supposed to have a better memory than the rest of the people on the planet. When you admit to the gaps, you admit that you're human. You're not pretending to know everything—even though it is your story. Maybe there are other versions of a particular event: you're just telling the one you have. Acknowledging the gaps keeps you honest as you write. It also creates a bond with your reader. Many people feel pain when they realize that details of vitally important memories have gone missing. They'll connect emotionally with your experience of trying to make sense of the past with only partial information.

Because not-remembering is such a common and charged human experience, it's just as useful for writing fiction. Everybody revisits certain memories: maybe for nostalgic reasons, maybe hoping for guidance, maybe because that's what they're trying to escape or because they're playing out some pattern that isn't actually a response to the current circumstances at all. What are your characters' cherished or haunting memories, and what in those memories do they not remember? You'll explore character in more depth in Session 7, "Tender Spots," so for now we'll just say that any prompt which deepens your understanding of yourself and your life is worth doing in the voice of your characters, as a way to understand who they are beyond the demands of the plot.

And, of course, since many fiction writers draw from their own lives, researching into your own memories gives you material to work with.

Make "not-remembering" part of your practice

As you make your way through the Writer Training, you'll probably find yourself writing "I don't remember" here and there. Before long it will become second nature to you to write what you don't know. You can always turn to these three words if you want to prod your imagination into a new perspective on your life.

So, if you feel bogged down during a writing prompt, start writing about what you don't remember. If there's an event, or a person, or a place you're working with that feels too neatly tied up or flat on the page, do an "I don't remember" for it. It's worth writing to this prompt again and again, even for the same event or place or person. Every time you do it, you'll find something new.

Recap

Congratulations! You've just completed Session 1 of the Writer Training. Since this is your introduction to the Imaginative Storm, let's recap.

In this first session, you practiced the three core principles of Imaginative Storm writing:

- Welcoming whatever your imagination comes up with
- Making a list
- Writing what you don't know

Plus:

- You've discovered the creative opportunities that await when you have absolutely no idea what you're going to write.
- You've learned how to let your imaginative mind lead the dance with your rational mind—and what interesting material that produces.
- You've realized that mess is currency, not a liability.
- You know how to storm random words into something meaningful and moving.
- You've experienced how storming your imagination makes the writing process intriguing and enjoyable.
- You're understanding that what you don't know has as much value as what you know.
- You're beginning to retrain your inner critic into your inner coach.
- And you have four pieces of material that you might use in something you write further down the line.

Sure, it takes practice to become comfortable letting your imagination get stormy and take the lead away from your rational mind. It's not something everyone can do fluently from a standing start, but as you integrate this work into your writing practice, you'll find that it's like learning to ride a bicycle. Suddenly you just get it. And you never lose it. You'll always be able to draw strength from the Imaginative Storm and stir things up when needed.

Now, here's your first "Surf the Storm" prompt, to do in the time before you begin Session 2, "Let Rip."

Surf the Storm

Prompt: Harvest words anywhere

Grab your notebook and pen and wander around your house looking for the words lurking everywhere: on packaging and labels, buttons on appliances, books and magazines, instruction leaflets, and so on. Create a list of the random words and phrases that catch your fancy, such as "no artificial anything" or "1 GAL" or "this side up."

You can harvest words anywhere. Try it on a road trip, dictating the words into your phone. Amuse yourself during a dull speech by jotting down random words (people will think you're taking notes). TV commercials may become a viewing pleasure—especially the overheated ones.

When you're ready to write, set the list of emotion words you created earlier in front of you, alongside the list of words you harvested. Pull up an emotion, or a mix of emotions. Feel the emotion in your body as intensely as you can.

Release any intention of what you're going to write, or any judgment of what you "should" write. Let your eyes drift over the list of found words until a word or phrase grabs you. Start there, and use as few or as many of the words you harvested as you please.

Set your timer **10** **and write**

When you're finished, read what you wrote aloud.

Write Playfully

When we put that zebra on a trapeze eating a pineapple, did you think, "How ridiculous!" Did you feel any inner resistance to following the prompt?

If you're just exploring writing as a creative pursuit, playfulness may have come easily to you. But if you aspire to be a serious writer, a "real" writer, a published writer—or you already are—that resistance might have been intense. Working with something as absurd as a zebra on a trapeze might seem to insult the seriousness of your commitment to writing—or, at best, it might just seem like a waste of time.

There are many activities in life in which heading straight for the goal is not the best route, and a bit of playfulness makes the end result way more satisfying. You can probably think of at least one. Well, writing is another.

Playfulness is the prep that brings freshness and spontaneity to your writing. It energizes your imagination, your writing, and most especially you. Playing when you write trains your body and your mind to weave unexpected words and ideas together across the wide range of your imagination rather than going down the same old fence-lined track. Playfulness teaches you to celebrate your originality, however bizarre it turns out to be.

Know that playfulness quickly gets easier as you work with Imaginative Storm prompts. The trick is to separate your attachment to the result from your commitment to the process. You can be serious about wanting to strengthen your writing chops, while knowing that being playful is the way to do it.

When you play, you're not attached to a result. You're not judging. You're enjoying the flow of the activity without worrying about whether you're doing it right. You don't have to be wild and crazy or ha-ha funny—though you might. You'll know you're playing if you feel a smile creeping across your face as you write.

When you stretch your imagination by urging it to push further, it's like stretching a muscle. Blood flows in, its range of movement grows, it gets stronger. Now it *wants* to do more! It's antsy for more challenges. How silly or extreme can you get? How far you can you take an idea or a metaphor?

Playfulness creates opportunities for fabulous mistakes. It gives you the confidence to include the weird things—the idiosyncrasies and quirks that bring your writing alive and give it your signature. You know those moments when you read another writer's work and say to yourself, "How did they think of that?!" Guess what: they probably didn't "think of it." It wasn't the result of willful effort. It just came to them because they'd trained their rational mind to welcome the gifts of their imagination.

This is what leads some of our participants to conclude that after Imaginative Storm, writer's block is a myth. It's a myth that might serve you short-term: if you want to think of yourself as a writer and you're not writing, then you must be suffering from writer's block. Only writers get writer's block, by definition! That feeds into another myth: that writers should be racked with struggle and angst if they're "real writers."

Myths aren't lies. They have truth to them—just not literal truth. It's true that there are days when nothing comes and "writer's block" feels like an ogre blocking your path. It's true that completing a writing project can be hard, and that every time you start a new one, you don't know if you can pull it off. The labor and the doubt and the apathetic days are real. What's not real is that you are powerless to do anything about them.

Write playfully! Delighting in words makes you want to play more with them. Experimenting with words expands your range. Enjoying your writing makes the labor pleasant. Surprising yourself with what you write makes the doubt at least temporarily irrelevant. And widening the path by giving your imagination more possibilities to explore makes the ogre of "writer's block" shrink to the size of a hamster.

"When we *imagine* anything, we are playing with images, combining them as they have never been combined before, perhaps not even in nature itself. Out of such playing with images came primitive ritual and the mythologies of early religion. Out of our playing with rocks and herbs and the mystery of fire came early science. Out of our playing with hollow reeds or tightened sinews or the beat of bone on deerskin came early music; musicians still "play" on their pianos or guitars. And out of our playing with words, with their sounds and shapes and rhythms and the images they conjured, came early poetry, so wonderful that in all parts of the world it seemed a kind of magic."

— John Frederick Nims, *Western Wind: An Introduction to Poetry*

Session 2:
Let Rip

In the previous session, "Spin the Kaleidoscope of Your Mind," you abandoned logic. In this session, you'll abandon moderation. Once again, you'll be writing what you may think you're not supposed to write.

When you set your imagination free from the constraints of reality and reason, you embraced the idea that what you were writing wasn't "serious." You knew this imaginative storm would blow over; you even put a time limit on it. You had the safety of knowing you'd be able to get back to rationality any time you wanted to. Did that freedom feel good—even if it was a bit unsettling at first? Did it make you laugh and give you energy? Did you feel your range of possibilities expanding?

In this session, you'll set your writing free in a different way. You'll feel the thrill of letting your opinions and passions run riot, beyond the bounds of what you're supposed to think and say. You'll throw caution and politeness to the wind. Forget about seeing both sides. Forget about being reasonable. Forget about being kind or fair. Forget about your dignity and what other people might think of you.

Rant! The more extreme, the better.

Most people, much of the time, don't say what they actually mean. It might be bad manners. It might sound harsh or crazy or politically incorrect. Also, you might feel a bit exposed when you really throw down. What if someone disagrees with you? Are you inviting criticism or argument? If you dislike conflict, you tend to soften your words.

In *Zen in the Art of Writing*, science fiction author Ray Bradbury writes:

> If you are writing without zest, without gusto, without love, without fun, you are only half a writer. . . . How long has it been since you wrote a story where your real love or your real hatred somehow got onto the paper? When was the last time you dared release a cherished prejudice so it slammed the page like a lightning bolt? What are the best things and the worst things in your life, and when are you going to get around to whispering or shouting them?

So, are you ready to throw lightning bolts onto paper? What do you really think? How do you really feel?

Seed the Storm

Prompt: Little white lies

To start off, let's look at what people really mean when they tell those little white lies you hear every day. They're so routine you hardly notice them: phrases like "He's very sweet" (in other words, "He's spineless and bores me to tears") or "Those shoes are pretty amazing" (in other words, "Those shoes are staggeringly ugly"). In the South, when someone feels the need to compliment an unremarkable baby, you might hear them say, "That's a real baby!"

Most people don't want to be hurtful or cause offense—there's a reason why good manners exist. But when you start writing, your default setting is often the same default setting you have for social situations. You write what you think people want to read. And then, when you assess the bland, inauthentic result, you feel frustrated and you don't quite know why.

So, we'll start by examining that default setting and having some fun with it. It's much more productive to laugh at your constraints than to get frustrated by them.

You'll begin by making a list of things you say to be polite: excuses or little white lies. Not things other people say. Things *you* say.

Set your timer (2) and make your list now

Did any of those surprise you? Sometimes you don't even realize you're not being entirely truthful. Most of us are very well trained.

Now comes the fun part. Take a few minutes to translate the phrases on your list into what you *really* want to say. Don't hold back. Do this out loud.

Here are some phrases and their translations from participants in our workshops that amused us:

"She's very caring."
Translation: Very nosy.

"I can't talk now, I have a meeting."
Translation: A meeting with my bed.

"How interesting."
Translation: That tells me a lot about you, and it's not good.

"I'm sure that's very reasonable."
Translation: You can be a slave to logic. Not me.

Once you become aware of how easily we socialized humans paper over the truth, you can play with evasions and white lies like these. When you portray a charged situation and have a character say something bland or mealy-mouthed, your reader will fill in for themselves what that character really wanted to say.

This is what screenwriters call subtext: a meaning that's carried by the words but is never spelled out. It lurks in the white space on the page. The character feels real because you sense them thinking, and the dissociation between what's said and what's not said creates tension. That gap between surface and subtext can be funny, or it can be threatening. (Think of all those silky-voiced film villains.) Either way, it's a source of energy.

But that's enough subtext for now. From here on, you are going to say exactly what you think. Loud and clear and as wild as you can make it.

Prompt: "I effing HATE . . ."

About 15 years ago, in a workshop in Galway, Ireland, a woman named Jane responded to an entirely different prompt by ranting about the revulsion, the visceral disgust, the outright nausea she felt when she saw ears poking through long straight hair. In 10 minutes of writing, she got up a real head of steam. It was hilarious. And even those of us who'd never thought about this before (translation: everybody else in the room) felt our own glimmers of disgust. We've never been able to see long straight hair in the same way again.

So, what bugs you? What infuriates you? What do you really loathe?

Before you start ranting, give yourself a list of possibilities. Big, important things or trivial things. Stay away from politics—most people already have their rant on that subject fully formed. Focus on things you hate that other people find normal, or don't notice, or maybe even love. Here are a few examples from our workshops:

Christmas music	*sugary breakfast cereal*
hugs from strangers	*old tea bags in the sink*
craft fairs	*"fashionably" frayed jeans*
the phrase "with an au jus"	*powerful perfume*
intentionally noisy cars	*bossy road junctions*

Now it's your turn. Feel free to include any of the items above if they make you crazy too.

Set your timer **(5)** **and make your list now**

Making a list like this gives you a running start before you dive into 10 minutes of joined-up writing. There's much less pressure in writing a list, and it's easier to choose something from a list than to come up with a topic cold. Use this technique whenever you like during the Writer Training, even if we don't ask you to.

Now, it's time to rant. Choose one of the items on your list that you effing hate and take a stand! It might go against something you've been taught your whole life. It might go against prevailing social currents or groupthink. It might seem completely idiotic. It might be a stand that would put you in danger if it went public. (Good news: it won't unless you want it to.)

Say it aloud and really feel it:

"I [effing] HATE . . ."
[insert your expletive of choice]

Don't compromise! Don't make allowances!

Set your timer (10) and rant now

When you're finished, read what you wrote aloud.

Most people find ranting a blast. But some people find it challenging, even upsetting, because—for whatever reason—they're used to keeping themselves on a tight rein. If this is you, try a few more rants. Give yourself permission to let fly. Say it aloud, and mean it: "I give myself permission to let fly!" Training on this prompt will make your writing more vivid and emotionally connected.

There's no energy in walking the fence—unless we feel the pressure of the wobbles. If you're writing a character who walks the fence, writing a rant as "research" will give you material for the wobbles.

You might have a nagging concern that your rant is objectionable or offensive. Don't worry: you don't ever have to share it. It was the truth of the moment, and that's valuable. You're training your inner critic to let you generate material without interfering (you'll assess it later). You're feeling what it's like to break out of the social straitjacket—and even if that's something you would never do in public, other people do. Maybe one day you'll create a character who uses that objectionable rant. A great example is Patricia Smith's poem "Skinhead," which she performed on Def Poetry Jam. You can find it on YouTube.

The James List: Unexpected loves

This is our first "James List," named for one of our participants, James Coats, who remarked that he'd enjoyed working with this prompt because it helped him appreciate the abundance of good feeling in his life. So, in every session from here on, you'll find a list-making prompt that creates a little breather in between longer pieces of writing.

This list will be the opposite of the last list you made. What things do you love that would surprise people? Things that other people hate, or look down on, or don't even notice.

Here are some examples from our workshops:

rats in the New York subway   *plastic flowers*
falling-down fences   *shoveling snow*
older women who dress in   *the feeling of your ears popping in*
   cloudy shades of gray   *an airplane*

Set your timer (5) and make your list now

When you're finished, read your list aloud.
Feel how much you love each of these things.

When you're out with friends, you might ask them the same question: "What do you love that other people hate or don't even notice?" They'll mention things they love that make you say, "Yes!

42

Me too!" They'll mention other things they love that make you say, "Seriously?"

You may be surprised by how you connect with another person's feeling of love, even if you'd never have imagined being able to feel love for that particular thing. In one workshop, a participant gushed about the sound of helicopter blades above the beach. Another spoke tenderly about cleaning the cat box, which transformed the experience from an unpleasant task into an act that's almost devotional.

When somebody loves something, it becomes lovable.

Prompt: "I effing LOVE . . ."

You've already thrown lightning bolts of loathing onto the page. Now, you'll throw lightning bolts of love.

We've encouraged you to crash opposites together: to express hate for what other people love, to express love for what other people hate. It's kind of delicious to go against the grain, and it frees you up. We'll explore this idea further in Session 10, "The Oxymoronic Inversion." For now, just notice the extra energy that a clash of expectations brings to your writing.

Choose an item from your James List—the more unexpected the better. Say it aloud and really feel it:

"I [effing] LOVE . . ."
[insert your expletive of choice]

Feel every ounce of your love for this thing. Luxuriate in it, delight in it, feel the sheer ecstasy of your love for this unlikely object of your affection.

Set your timer  **and rant now**

When you're finished, read what you wrote aloud.

Many people feel a social pressure to be positive and cheery even when that's not their reality. We played with that in the "Seed the Storm" prompt. Because of that conditioning, it can be difficult to really let go when you talk about loving something, because you're so used to being in the temperate, superficial zone. That's why we set the negative rant prompt first—it's actually easier for most people. Interestingly, stirring up all that energy, by writing a rant with teeth and bite and force, often releases something unexpectedly tender and vulnerable in your positive material. You could say that the prep work of a negative rant is the medicine to alleviate superficiality.

Rants are prompts you can do again and again. If you're working on something and inspiration just isn't coming, write a rant. It'll get your juices flowing, and you may even end up using it, as Allegra did in her novel *A Stolen Summer*, when she gave two random rants of her own to the two main characters.

Surf the Storm

Prompt: Go big or go home

You know what they say: "Go big or go home." In other words, do it full-throttle or don't do it at all.

That's what we've encouraged you to do as you let rip on the page. Now, as you go about your days before starting the next session, think about times when you wish you'd gone bigger—or when you wish you'd gone home.

When you've settled on an incident you want to explore,

Set your timer (10) **and write**

When you're finished, read what you wrote aloud.

Write Without Trying

The Imaginative Storm technique is built on the premise that *trying* to write well is a major obstacle to writing well. Maybe you've already experienced this in your own writing. It's frustrating. It saps your confidence and your motivation and your energy. You start to think, "If I can't write well, no matter how hard I try, I guess I can't write."

Your problem is not that you can't write. You can. After teaching writing workshops to hundreds of people, we can say that for certain. Almost everybody, given the right techniques and encouragement, can touch a reader with their words.

The problem is the trying, because the effort stiffens the words. Here's why.

First, you're not in the flow of the moment. You have your eyes on the outcome, not the process, so your hopes and fears are jostling around in the forefront of your mind. You hope it will get published. You're afraid you can't pull it off. Added to that, you're worrying about what other people will think, and that makes you self-conscious.

Second, you're judging what you write *as* you write, so you're in your critical mind, not your creative mind. (There is a time for judging what you write, and it isn't now.) When you're concerned about the individual words hitting the page, your writing can't pick up momentum. You're constantly fighting the gremlin in the back of your mind that whispers, "That's not good enough. You can't do this."

Your creative mind thinks, "Why should I put myself through this?" So it packs up for the day.

That gremlin is your inner critic—which we'll examine in more detail later. It's trying to help you, but it thinks you want to write well every time you put words on a page. You have to teach it that that's not how this creativity thing works.

Third, when you're trying to produce good writing, you're often trying to mimic other writing you think is good. In other words, you're trying to write like somebody else, maybe even like multiple somebody elses. So it's hardly surprising that you can't hear your own voice in the din, and you'd feel that "finding your voice" is a difficult and desperate necessity. Maybe, like so many writers, you've said it out loud: "I have to find my voice." There's a lot of "trying" embedded in that sentence. We'd say you don't have to find it. All you have to do is stop trying to write well, and it will come out.

Did you rant fiercely, angrily, sarcastically, calmly, or with biting logic? Did you enthuse with passion, with tenderness, with joy, with serene certainty? That was your voice, right there. No searching required.

We asked you to rant early in the Writer Training because when you get up a head of steam, the words pour out without effort. Now you know what it feels like to write without trying. Other prompts might not open the floodgates so wide, but whenever you feel that flow starting, go with it. Don't hold it back because you had some other intention for what you were going to write.

That's not to say the floodgates are supposed to open every time the timer starts. They don't. But you up your chances of even a short little burst if you allow yourself to feel your way into what you write, rather than trying to accomplish a task.

But what if you just go blank? You set the timer, and nothing comes.

It happens. Don't let yourself fall back into that "I can't write!" panic. There's nothing wrong with what's happening—or not happening. There's nothing wrong with you.

If your mind starts to churn with thoughts like "What should I write? What would a good writer write? I want to do this right," and so on, put that on the page. Write, "I don't know what to write! This is idiotic! What the hell am I doing here?" The thoughts themselves tie you up, but when you write them down, you sap their power because—guess what?—you're actually writing something! Here's a great example, a haiku written by our participant Patty Graves (she actually wrote three haikus in the 10 minutes):

Nothing is working!
Foreboding of my failures
Swallowing me whole.

Other participants find that once they break through a barrier by just writing anything, the piece suddenly morphs into something pretty intense. We're not quite sure why that happens, but we've seen it happen countless times.

Stay relaxed and stay open—even if you don't burst out of the starting gate when the timer starts. Sink into the emotions that the prompt calls up in you. Let your eyes roam over your lists of words. Close your eyes and let your imagination take you somewhere. Ask yourself what you don't remember, what wasn't there, what else could have happened.

Noodle around with whatever words do come. And if you still have nothing when the timer pings, that's just what happened this time. Part of the Writer Training is learning not to force it.

The moments in your writing that take you by surprise are the moments of spark and energy. You can't try to surprise yourself, just like you can't give yourself a surprise birthday party. But you can make a surprise party possible: tell people it's your birthday, stick to your routine, don't make other plans. Equally, you can make surprise in your writing possible by giving yourself prompts that send you into unfamiliar territory.

Stay curious. When you're curious, you forget about writing well.

You just want to see what comes out. Curiosity and the inner critic cannot coexist.

As you become more comfortable writing to Imaginative Storm prompts, you'll turn toward patience rather than effort. You'll build up trust in the process. Often you won't start writing immediately—but you'll have confidence that if you sit with the prompt, most of the time, something will come.

"For instance, the previous run-on sentence is a sentence fragment, and it happened in part because of the really nice time my body was having making this lavender Le Pen make the loop-de-looping we call language. I mean writing. The point: I'd no sooner allow that fragment to sit there like a ripe zit if I was typing on a computer. And consequently, some important aspect of my thinking, particularly the breathlessness, the accruing syntax, the not quite articulate pleasure that evades or could give a f*** about the computer's green corrective lines (how they injure us!) would be chiseled, likely with a semicolon and a proper predicate, into something correct, and, maybe, dull. To be sure, it would have less of the actual magic writing is, which comes from our bodies, which we actually think with, quiet as it's kept."

— Ross Gay, *The Book of Delights*

Session 3:
Common Senses

In this session, you'll be working with your five primary senses: sight, hearing, smell, taste, and touch. You'll also explore others that aren't so often mentioned, such as proprioception, the sense of your body in space. And did you know that when you hold someone close, your heartbeats synchronize? The sense of another person's bodily rhythms doesn't even have a name.

Then there are senses that are not common to us all—and some people don't believe they even exist. Are you sensitive to the vibes of certain places? Are you good at sensing what weather is coming? Do you feel the emotions of people around you? Some people have an excellent sense of direction, which might rely on visual clues or the memory of a map but could also be an echo of how birds and butterflies navigate.

Think back to the last session, "Let Rip." When you turned the emotional dial up high, did you notice how your emotions informed your bodily senses? Did your heart race, your pen move faster or press harder, your legs tense up or relax, your neck soften or strain forward or back? Did you hear the noises you know were there, such as traffic or the refrigerator turning on, or did they disappear? Did your mouth taste bitter or sweet?

Practice that self-awareness when you can. It's your authenticity meter: when you feel the emotion in your body, you know you're writing into the truth of what you want to say.

It works the other way around, too. You might already know that just making the physical motion of smiling makes you feel happy; it's an automatic physiological response, because your body knows that happiness is what smiling expresses. The amazing thing is that you also feel happy when you see someone else smile. You can't help smiling yourself, and you feel a true jolt of happiness. When you see someone tense up with anger or fear, you tense up. In both cases, the mirror neurons in your brain are transferring the emotions of another creature into you.

This is what happens when a reader responds to your writing; they're responding to the character on the page the same way they'd respond to a real person. Their mirror neurons fire when they recognize specific sensations or emotions or predicaments as part of their own experience.

It's the specificity that creates the connection—the uncommonness, you might say, that creates the commonality.

Seed the Storm

Prompt: Sensing without sight

Humans rely heavily on the faculty of sight, and it's tightly tied in with your rational mind. If you're used to being able to see, being unable to see disorients you. You feel unsure, even unsafe. When you're disoriented, when you feel unsure, you tend to drop out of a judging frame of mind. You look for guidance, search for clues. You're open to what you don't know.

So, closing your eyes is a valuable and easy technique for quieting your rational mind. It gives your imagination room to explore and sharpens your other senses.

Here's what you'll do:

Set your timer, then close your eyes. Trace your fingers across whatever is within reach. What feels familiar? What feels unfamiliar? Do some textures draw you in, some repel you?

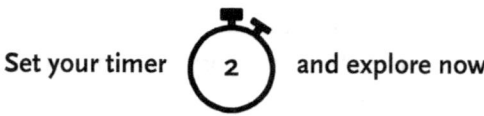

Set your timer (**2**) **and explore now**

Now, pick up your pen and write about what you felt. What surprised you?

Set your timer (**5**) **and write now**

When you're finished, read what you wrote aloud.

Did you find that you wrote more slowly to this prompt? Your hand as you wrote may have been mirroring the movement of your hands as you explored the familiar territory that became unfamiliar when you closed your eyes. When you're curious, you often move more slowly.

Throughout the Writer Training, we'll ask you to look at the familiar from an unfamiliar perspective. We'll encourage you to write what you don't know rather than what you know.

When you closely investigate the elements of a scene with senses other than sight, you zoom in on specific details instead of just taking a general snapshot. What is that edge? How hard can I push before that mug falls over? What sound does the desk make when I tap it? Is the fabric of that curtain rough or just nubbly? This kind of close attention gives your writing an intensity even if the words aren't trying to convey emotion at all. This may be because to pay such close attention, you must care.

A further benefit of this prompt is that you build trust in yourself. If something wasn't interesting, you moved on and found something that was. You trusted that new discoveries would come, and they did. You weren't contorting your rational mind with dilemmas about what you should or shouldn't touch, or whether you were doing it right. Pen-down fast writing isn't the only way to silence your inner critic; prompts like this help retrain your inner critic into your inner coach. You're giving it different standards to uphold: not "is this written well," but "am I being patient, am I being curious, am I being open to what I don't know and to what I don't expect?"

You can return to this slow-paced, sense-focused mindset whenever it feels right. Even if we don't suggest it, try closing your eyes at the beginning of a prompt before you start to write.

Prompt: Emotion in the body

In the previous prompt, you felt the external world. Now, you'll explore how your body responds to your inner feelings.

In Session 1, you created your own list of emotion words. Look back at that list, or use the list below, adding some more emotion words of your own.

joy	*fear*	*embarrassment*
boredom	*frustration*	*angst*
hope	*grief*	*uncertainty*
despair	*tenderness*	*disgust*
contentment	*excitement*	*satisfaction*
pleasure	*sadness*	*anger*

Now, it's time to write.

Let your eyes roam over the words until they land on an emotion that you can bring up right now. Close your eyes and think about a time when that emotion was intense. Visualize the place, the scene, the action. Hear any noises or words that were said. Take time to feel the emotion flood your body.

When you're ready to write, describe what your body feels like—from head to feet, or feet to head. Starting from your core and moving outward, or starting at your fingertips and toes and moving in. Scan your entire body and pick up every little sensation that you possibly can.

Don't name the emotion as you write. Just describe the physical sensations. Because this is not something most of us are used to doing, you'll probably find yourself moving to what you thought or what you saw—but keep bringing yourself back to how your body feels.

Set your timer (**10**) **and write now**

When you're finished, read what you wrote aloud.

Most people are amazed by the emotional power of what they write to this prompt. As you describe bodily sensations, the emotion re-ignites even more intensely. It's not just memory.

You can access this direct emotional power easily when you move your focus from thinking to feeling. Give yourself over to your physical perceptions of your outer and inner worlds.

The James List: Sounds you love

Sounds have tremendous emotional power. Even ordinary sounds can be precious, such as the sound of your spouse returning home or your child's footsteps running down the hall.

What sounds do you love? Make a list.

Set your timer 5 and make your list now

When you're finished, read your list aloud—and notice the sensations in your body while you name the sounds you love.

In the previous session, we suggested that when you get together with friends, you invite everyone to make a list of unexpected loves. You might do another list of just sounds. Making lists like these reminds us of the simple riches we have in our lives. They also bring up a rush of affection for people who appreciate things and activities that are rarely loved, such as cleaning the cat box. For example, one Imaginative Storm participant included the sound of a lawnmower on her list—and even those of us who will never love that sound thought of the delicious smell of newly cut grass.

If you're writing fiction, you can give some of the more unusual items on these lists to your characters. It's a great way to anchor them in their own individual reality. It's also a terrific way to generate dialogue.

Prompt: Activate your nondominant senses

In the first prompt of this session, you closed your eyes and let your fingers investigate your immediate environment. To gather material for your last piece of the session, you'll repeat the experience—but more so.

Here's what you'll do:

- Stand up and close your eyes.
- Start moving slowly around the room. Shuffle rather than walk so you don't hurt yourself.
- Listen to the sounds. Sniff the objects you come across.
- Feel the air on your skin. Taste it on your tongue.

Set your timer (5) **and explore now**

Keep going after the timer pings, if you want to.

Did you notice how your other senses grew more acute when sight was taken out of the mix? How curious and hungry for information they became?

Did you notice how proprioception came to the forefront of your awareness? You might have felt unsteady without your eyes to guide you, as gravity pulled you to earth. You might also have lost a sense of which way you were facing in relation to where you started.

Did your sense of scale veer unexpectedly? Maybe you ran your fingers along an edge and wondered when it would ever end—an edge that when you see it doesn't seem particularly long. Your eyes travel much faster than your fingers, especially when your fingers are being careful, and your eyes normally give you a fairly two-dimensional representation, an overview without much detail. Sightless "seeing" makes you far more aware of dimensionality and concreteness, and of subjective qualities like temperature. Depending on the substance they're made of, two objects next to each other might feel different when touched: one warm, the other cool.

Now it's time to write.

You're not going to describe this experience. Instead, it's your prep work. Now that your senses are newly activated, imagine yourself into another room, a room you know well—not the room you're in right now. Experience that room in your imagination with all your senses alive to what they might find, just like you experienced this room in reality.

Then, put pen to paper and describe that room to a person who has never had a sense of sight. Any visual description you include won't mean anything to them. Tell them what they will hear, what they will smell, what they will taste, what they will touch. What might surprise them? What might catch them unawares or make them feel unsafe? What might give them comfort?

Set your timer (**10**) **and write now**

When you're finished, read what you wrote aloud.

Taking sight out of the equation gives you material for a much more immediate and emotional experience of a memory. When you recount a memory according only to what you saw, you and your reader both are watching the scene like you watch a video. You're not in it; you're a spectator. But when you generate the material without using the dominant sense of sight, you find ways of bringing yourself, and your reader, right there into that moment.

Surf the Storm

Prompt: An uncommon sense

Have you ever felt the energy of a place strongly? Some people would call it the vibes of a place. Did an emotion arise inexplicably that seemed to be somehow connected to the place? Did you imagine you heard things, saw things, felt things, smelled or tasted things? Did your body move, or want to move, in a way that wasn't dictated by your conscious mind?

If you've never experienced anything like this, consider what other "extra" sense you might have—or what it might be like if you had one.

Set your timer  **and write**

When you're finished, read what you wrote aloud.

Write Without Criticism

Have you ever heard a voice in your head telling you that you're a hopelessly bad writer? Most people call that voice their inner critic. You'll hear people say they want to silence their inner critic. Many writing coaches go so far as to advise killing off your inner critic.

We look at it differently. That voice in your head is not trying to undermine you. It's actually trying to help. You want to do things well. You want praise for your efforts. Nobody wants to be dissed or laughed at if their work isn't up to scratch. The inner critic is there to uphold standards.

And what kind of thanks does it get? A gag order, and threats on its life!

The inner critic attacks you and gets frustrated because it doesn't understand how to do its job—like a sheepdog that nips at people's ankles because it doesn't have any sheep to herd. It's smart, it has good instincts, and it wants to work. It just needs training.

Your inner critic needs standards to uphold. There's nothing wrong with having standards: for social behavior, driving, many activities. You just want to be supported, not chastised, as you go about meeting them, and you don't want to be held to a standard that doesn't apply. A new driver is not doing it wrong because they can't drive Formula One.

Your inner critic needs to learn what standards should be applied at the various stages of creativity. And if it didn't start off with good role models, it may have to learn to praise as well as criticize. Top athletes and businessmen have coaches to tell them what they're doing right as well as what they can improve. In the course of the Writer Training, you'll turn your inner critic into your inner coach.

When you're first generating material, you're looking for good material rather than "good writing." The point of a 10-minute time limit is to train the inner critic not to look for "good writing," since obviously nothing generated that quickly can reach that standard. (That's what most inner critics think to begin with. By the time you finish the Writer Training, yours may think differently.) So, what do you want it to look for?

- That the work exists. There are actually words on the page.
- Any word, phrase, image, or thought that has energy.
- Anything that feels like you've never said it or thought it quite that way before.

If you get one little moment that pops in the entire 10-minute piece, you've more than succeeded. Your inner coach can whoop and holler—or if it's not that demonstrative, it can just give you a little pat on the back.

Here are some more things your inner coach can look for:

- Will I be able to read my writing?
- Am I letting my imagination take the lead?
- Am I experimenting and exploring and playing?
- Am I letting the work be messy?
- Am I sounding like me, or trying to sound like someone else?
- Am I remembering not to criticize myself?

You may have already noticed that your inner critic is not as fierce as it used to be. It doesn't need to be, because it's learning that at this stage of the proceedings, its job is to support you as you work to make yourself a better writer, not to judge whether you've succeeded yet. It may realize that something is coming into being—something it can exercise its critical faculties on later down the line. If at some point you decide to work up your material into a piece that might go out into the world, your inner critic will be your ally in making your work as good as it can possibly be.

Even then, it may need more training. You want it speaking to you in a way that's helpful, not discouraging. The two rules of editing are:

1. Praise
2. Ask questions

Give yourself kudos for any moment in your writing, however small, that you're genuinely proud of. As for the rest, don't stop at "This bit isn't working" or "That's a cliché," because then your inner critic might fall back into its old bad habits and follow up with "You're a lousy writer." Get that question in first! Ask yourself, "How can I fix this?" And when you're fixing it, tell your inner critic to put its coach hat back on again. Let any new words flow without judgment. Try a few different fixes. You can assess them later.

"It's incredibly comfortable and nice when you can look at your own work and say to yourself, 'I did a good job.' And then you let it go, because anything else is going to make you crazy, and anything else, you're going to be trying to impress people who don't even like you. That's the truth! You have to be very careful of letting people who not only don't know you, but don't understand you, don't like you . . . you can't let those people determine who you are."

— Nikki Giovanni

Session 4:
Go There

Everything happens somewhere. Locations aren't just backdrops to a story—they're an integral part of how you tell it. The more firmly your story is anchored in physical space, the more alive and authentic it will feel.

In the last session, you used your senses to examine your immediate environment. As you moved around your room with your eyes closed, perhaps you touched a loose nail, sniffed the cloth on the back of a chair, listened to the breeze outside, tasted a clean knife. Did you notice how your sensory engagement made your ordinary circumstances more vivid and intriguing?

The way you describe a place conveys far more than just information. Surroundings shape people's behavior, influence their comfort level, change their mood. A place can be a paradise or a prison—or maybe both at the same time. Sunlight through a window can be warm and cheerful, or harsh and glaring. A layer of dust can convey neglect, or other priorities, or it could be thick as velvet and soft with good memories.

If you studied literature in school, you were probably taught to look at this aspect of storytelling in an analytical way: "See how the author reflects the protagonist's emotional state by describing the quality of the light," or "Notice how Fitzgerald uses the green light on Daisy's dock to represent Gatsby's romantic longing." Having learned that way, you might think you're supposed to build the scene in the same way: that you should have an agenda of emotion to convey, and use your judgment to choose the best carrier for it. We'd bet the farm that Fitzgerald didn't get that green light by thinking, "Hmm, what object can I put in the description of the lake to represent Gatsby's romantic longing?" That perfect fusion of description and emotion has to arise organically.

So, how do you make that happen?

The key is to build up your settings as you build up the story. It's not something you do separately, like: I'll write what happened, and then I'll go back and describe the curtains. When you build up the details of a location in sync with the story, your imagination will naturally settle on elements of the place that reflect how the character feels, how they think about themselves, what they fear or hope for, what they think they should or shouldn't do or wish they had or hadn't done. You'll find details that convey far more emotion and symbolic meaning than you could ever put into words.

Seed the Storm

Prompt: Emotional details of a place

In the previous session, you explored how emotions express themselves in your body. Now, you'll locate those emotions outside your body, in the details of a place.

Recall a place that at some point in your life you had a powerful emotional connection with—either positive or negative. For example, a childhood bedroom, a work site, or a room in which you received life-changing news.

Take a few minutes to visualize that place as fully as you can, and list as many details of that place as you can.

Set your timer (**5**) **and make your list now**

Did your imagination rev up as you remembered detail after detail? Did any of the details make emotions bubble up in your memory?

Now, connect emotions to the details on your list. For example, let's say you were working construction in a half-built mall. The endless piles of sheetrock disappearing into the gloom made you feel trapped on a hamster wheel. The political propaganda your co-worker left in your car made you feel you didn't belong there. The tuna sandwich you had for lunch made you feel loved, because your girlfriend made it for you exactly the same every day, just the way you like it.

You can use your list of emotion words as prompts, if you like. But as in this example, emotions don't have to be single words. Just make notes about how each detail made you feel.

As you do this, you may recall feeling an emotion in that place that doesn't attach to any of the details you listed. Imagine yourself back in that place and see if you can locate another detail that feels connected to that emotion, and add it to your list.

Don't worry about creating a one-to-one correlation between details and emotions. Many details might connect to the same emotion, and some details might bring up multiple emotions.

Keep this as note-taking, not joined-up writing. Take longer than 5 minutes if you like.

Set your timer (**5**) **and make notes**

Recalling details and emotional engagement in this disjointed way jogs your memory out of its usual track. It gets you out of your official version of your past. It's a kind of research—and research is a very important part of writing. Not all writing is a draft. Research into your own memories and life experience is as important as, if not more important than, the kind you do in libraries or on Google.

Prompt: The negative space

In the "I don't remember" prompt in Session 1, you wrote about what wasn't there in your memory. Here, you'll write about what wasn't there in a place. Focusing on the negative space puts you back in the moment, in the flow of life as you lived it.

Review the list of corresponding details and emotions you just created, and bring that place to mind one more time. As you describe it in joined-up writing, focus on *what wasn't there*.

Set your timer (10) **and write now**

When you're finished, read what you wrote aloud.

Was the negative space in your description a lack—something you wished was there—or was it a release from something you'd left behind? Did you find that the elements of the place that *were* there became linked to what was absent?

Did writing about what wasn't there in that place open up imaginative possibilities of how things could have gone differently? Did

65

your mind go to something that could have happened but didn't, or something you thought might happen in the future? After all, no chain of events is inevitable. It only seems that way in retrospect.

It sometimes happens that when you turn to the joined-up writing in this prompt, you use surprisingly few of the details on the original list. Why would that be? Our theory is that your rational mind looks at a memory as if through a camera, but when you return to the same scene from an emotional perspective, the focus shifts away from the visual sense. Details that your less dominant senses were aware of come to the forefront.

Sounds and smells rarely feature on people's original lists, but they often appear in the joined-up writing. You'll explore sounds and smells further in the "Surf the Storm" prompt at the end of this session.

The James List: Objects with a personality

Many inanimate objects have a personality. Have you ever seen those lovely animations of toasters? Many people have tender relationships with stuffed animals, vehicles, vacuum cleaners, and all kinds of other objects. And then there's that cat toy that always trips you up—sneaky, vicious thing!

Make a list of objects you have an emotional connection with—friend or foe. Don't let the word "object" limit you—you might have a guardian tree, or a comforting vista, or a welcoming stretch of road. It might be a building, or even a city. For example, in Madrid, the crosswalk signs have a picture of two people walking or waiting to walk, instead of just one—which makes Madrid itself seem sociable and warm.

Set your timer (5) **and make your list**

Try playing with this idea further and fleshing out the personality of one or more of the objects on your list. Ask it some questions:

- What does it want?
- What is it afraid of?
- What is its chief complaint?
- What does it love?

Perhaps you're working on a story and there's an object in it that carries meaning. For example, Mom's diamond ring: who gets it when she dies? Ask it: whose finger does it want to be on? Am I wrong to sell the ring to pay the rent? Well, what does it think? When you use questions like these to give an object a personality, you'll generate material you'd never have gotten any other way.

Use these questions, and others like them, for your flesh-and-blood characters as well. We'll explore that further in Session 7, "Tender Spots."

Prompt: Infuse a setting with story

Places carry the weight of things that have happened there, of the emotions people have felt there. In this prompt, you'll discover one way to tap into a place's cultural and personal significance.

Here's what you'll do:

Choose another location—not the same one you wrote about in the first prompt. A place you know well, which has meaning for you. Take as much time as you need to bring it vividly to mind.

Then set your timer and describe that place, focusing on what was out of place, unfinished, or in disrepair.

Set your timer (10) and write now

When you're finished, read what you wrote aloud.

If something is unfinished, there was once some intention by somebody to finish it. If something is in disrepair, that collapse has been allowed to happen. If something is out of place, some chain of events has led to this anomaly: why is it out of place, and who says what its right place would be?

Details like these also reflect the state of mind, the emotions, or the life circumstances of the characters who inhabit these environments. Think of the many stories that could be conveyed by a broken pane of glass.

Do you know the Japanese concept of *wabi sabi*: the beauty of things that are imperfect? Maybe because the thing is handmade, and it carries the story of its making. Or maybe because it's damaged, and it carries the story of what happened to it.

Entropy is the tendency of all things to fall out of what we consider their "correct" state of being and into a state of random organization. Entropy doesn't take long to assert itself. The atoms of your coffee mug are in one fixed arrangement, which is, statistically, a vanishingly small percentage of all possible arrangements of those atoms. How incredibly unlikely it is that they should stay in that one arrangement! Of course, they don't. The mug gets chipped. The color fades or stains. To our minds, this means something.

In reality, all existence is in flux. Atoms are constantly finding new patterns of organization, which we interpret as damage and disrepair, growth and decay. In making things and shaping nature to our aesthetic or practical desires, we humans try to control the processes of growth and decay. But eventually every palace or hut, skyscraper or garden, cruise missile or coffee mug, will disappear back into the tangle of nature.

Surf the Storm

Prompt: Tune in to your environment

Walk around the rooms of your house and notice the differences in sound and sound quality, in smells, in air quality. Take notes.

At another time, sit in some outdoor location for 20 minutes and list all the sounds you hear and the scents you smell. Staying in one place silently for a long time enables you to notice the subtleties of atmosphere that aren't immediately apparent.

See if you can keep this awareness over the course of a day. It won't be constant, as your mind will be occupied with many other things, but whenever you can, tune in to your environment again: when you're waiting in the supermarket checkout line, in the dentist's office, at a red light. Use the voice memo on your phone to take notes if you're in a situation where you can't write.

After doing this, you'll be far more aware of sound and smell than you're used to being—and maybe more aware of other details as well. Aspects of experience that ordinarily seem trivial take on importance—not just the culturally designated fabulous things, like the hoot of an owl, but the sound of wheels on asphalt or the different sounds rain makes on wood and on metal.

A friend of ours who lived on the west coast of Ireland lost her sense of smell after an illness. She could hardly bear to walk on the beach anymore, because without smell, she said, it was like watching the beach on television. She didn't feel like she was really there. It wasn't long before she moved to the city.

Isn't it amazing how much you're not aware of most of the time? Ask yourself some questions:

- Is there a difference in my perceptions between daytime and nighttime?
- Is there a difference in what I perceive according to my mood?
- Do some of these sounds and smells influence my mood subconsciously, even when I'm not fully aware of them?
- Do my feelings about these sounds and smells change because I'm becoming aware of them?

By bringing these subconscious perceptions into consciousness, you're training yourself to be more aware generally. Maybe you notice that your feet are a bit cold even though you've come indoors, because the house is chillier than the outdoors—it must be spring. Those cold feet, contrasted with the warm mug in your hands and counterpointed by the sound of the refrigerator cycling off, give continuity to a scene.

Write whatever you like, based on this experience of becoming more aware of sounds and smells.

Set your timer (**10**) **and write**

When you're finished, read what you wrote aloud.

Write What You Don't Know

We'll guess that before you began the Writer Training, you mostly wrote what you knew. You thought of a story and sat down to write it. Maybe you embarked on a memoir, since you've had a pretty interesting life, and started putting the interesting bits into words. You heeded those writing teachers who tell you to "write what you know."

Probably the writing didn't come out on the page the way you thought it would. Maybe it felt stale, or dull, or somehow inauthentic when you read it over. But it didn't feel dull or inauthentic in your mind, so what happened?

Your mind likes to make sense of things. It makes connections, and patterns of cause-and-effect. Your memory tidies up experience into stories, erasing the inconvenient bits that undermine the judgment it's decided on. But when you read a story with everything wrapped up neatly like this, something feels false. As a reader, you're not engaged. Your mirror neurons aren't firing, because you're not recognizing real human experiences in the words you're reading— even if *you* wrote them. So why would this happen?

When you're living life, all kinds of things are happening that you aren't aware of. Zillions of possibilities exist in every direction. Only in retrospect do you have a clear concept of what happened, and why, and how you feel about it. So, when you're writing about a past event and wanting a reader to connect with it, you have to find a way of getting yourself back to that moment-to-moment uncertainty. You have to travel back to the present of your past.

Our minds like to make us comfortable, and they like to make us right—or at least, excuse us for doing wrong. Our memories make adjustments to the reality of what happened. We edit out the messy bits, consciously or subconsciously. This isn't a fault or a failing—it's a normal human process. Most of us aren't even aware that it's occurred until we challenge our tidy version of events by asking ourselves questions like: What do I not remember? What wasn't there? What was I afraid of? What did I *really* want?

You may feel your rational mind resisting this turn back into uncertainty. It's already done all that wrapping up! Does this mean that the wrappings are somehow wrong—that your interpretations and judgments and even memories of fact are not correct? Well, that might be the case for any particular event, or it might not. You won't know until you let your imagination investigate questions that your rational mind won't ask on its own. You may have to push yourself to be open to those questions.

Don't discount your rational mind. It does this wrapping up for a very good reason: to make order out of chaos and keep you sane. In the past, as you wrote, it may have turned away from shadowy areas of uncertainty, because it wanted to hold on to what it knew. But it also likes to expand the borders of what it knows, so you can enlist it in exploring other possibilities. And best of all, it will enjoy making new interpretations and new judgments that include the gems you unearth from the present of your past.

We're skirting the borders of psychotherapy here. Therapy is not the goal of the Writer Training—though you will finish it with more self-knowledge than you had when you started. But writers are psychologists. Before the disciplines of psychology and psychotherapy were even invented, people turned to novels to understand human nature and get some ideas about how to navigate life. That's the tradition all writers are working in, however far they depart from realism. Human experience is your subject matter—and what better specimen do you have for investigating human nature than you?

You don't have to throw all your certainties out the window. Let's say you know for sure that you're walking west because it's 5 p.m. and the sun is in your eyes. Okay—but what are you not seeing because the sun is blinding you? What are you not aware of because you're thinking about dinner? Your certainties might not be inaccurate. They might just be incomplete.

Try looking at things you take for granted from a different perspective. Let's say you're five feet tall, so, as an adult human, you think of yourself as on the small side. Now stand over an ant colony. Are you still small? In *Gulliver's Travels*, when Gulliver goes to Lilliput, he's a giant because the people are the size of mice. Then he goes to Brobdingnag, where the people are gigantic and he's, relatively, the size of a Lilliputian. Two centuries later, Einstein imagined himself so small he could chase a beam of light—which led him to the special theory of relativity.

Your imagination is bored by what you know. If you've ever tried to write a book about your area of expertise, you probably encountered this problem. It seemed like a great idea, but the writing was just a slog, like one of those "What I Did Over My Vacation" school essays. So, even if your project is something factual or scientific, you'll need to find a way of writing what you don't know in order to engage your imagination, energize yourself, and put verve into the words on the page. Can you find a new angle on the material? Can you question your way of doing things: is your method really the best? Can you imagine what it might be like to teach someone who's just not getting it?

So, "I don't know" is not a lack. It's a realm that is always there for you to explore and to draw from. What you don't know today is there for you to discover in your writing. And when you know that, there will be another "I don't know" beyond it.

Do you know Tennyson's poem "Ulysses"? Ulysses is a veteran of the Trojan War, who wandered for 10 years as he tried to get back home. Now, in his old age, he feels dull and stale at home. He's bored of the everyday round, and he longs to set sail again. And while he's walking around his kingdom, thinking about what to do next, he says:

> I am a part of all that I have met
> Yet all experience is an arch wherethrough
> Gleams that untraveled world whose margin fades
> Forever and forever as I move.

You could think of your own untraveled world as your unthought thoughts and your unchallenged memories. The parts of your imagination and lived experience that await your exploration in writing—whose end is never in sight.

"No tears in the writer, no tears in the reader. No surprise for the writer, no surprise for the reader."

— Robert Frost, "The Figure a Poem
Makes," in *Collected Poems*

Session 5:
Elemental Alchemy

So far, you've tuned in to your imagination, your passions, your body, and your surroundings. In this session, you'll move out further, into the natural world.

When we talk about the natural world, we're usually thinking about deer and forests and beaches and thunder. Most people conceive of nature as something "out there"—there's the natural world and the human world, and they aren't the same. But when you stop to think about it, we ourselves are part of nature. Nature made us, and everything we make has its origin in the natural world.

Nature is constantly transforming: predators digest prey, plants feed on sunlight, water breaks down rock, fungus re-creates organic matter. The skin on your arm today is not the skin you touched a month ago. In the previous session, we asked you to describe a place focusing on what was unfinished or in disrepair. That was the evidence of a never-ending natural process expressing itself in what we think of as the man-made world.

The medieval alchemists sought to transform lead into gold. They sought to change something heavy, dull, and ordinary into something precious and gleaming. Did they succeed? Who knows—but let's say they did. Writing is a similar kind of alchemy. In the secret laboratory of the mind, writers apply the flame of imagination to the elements of ordinary life and transform them into a precious offering.

Seed the Storm

Prompt: Things that come from nature

The philosopher Marshall McLuhan said that we will never know who discovered water, but we can be sure it was not a fish—because a fish takes water for granted. One goal of the Writer Training is to hone your awareness of aspects of existence that you might take for granted.

Look around the environment you're in and make a list of things you see that come from nature.

As you were making your list, you probably realized that everything comes from nature in some way. The metals that make up your computer were mined from the earth. Your furniture and paper came from trees. The plaster on your walls is pulverized stone. The mug holding your coffee was once clay. Your wool sweater once warmed a sheep; your T-shirt grew in a field. The oil that made the plastic clothes hangers in your closet lay underground for millions of years.

Start with the words "Everything is _____" and choose an element to fill in the blank. Here are the four elements of the Western tradition:

earth   air   fire   water

Look back at the list you just made if you like—or not. Let your writing take you where it pleases.

Set your timer (5) **and write now**

When you're finished, read what you wrote aloud.

You can try this prompt four times, if you're so inspired. The more you look for commonality, the more you see how everything in our universe is interconnected.

Prompt: At one with an element

In this prompt, you'll write about a time when you felt yourself at one with an element. You can interpret that however you please.

This time, we'll use the six elements of the Chinese tradition. Here they are:

earth   air   fire   water   wood   metal

Let your imagination take you back to a time when you felt yourself at one with one of these elements. If something doesn't come immediately, just sit with it; trust that something will come. When it does, let your imagination flood your body with the feeling of earth, or air, or fire, or water, or metal, or wood. Let the element permeate your emotions as you write.

Set your timer (10) **and write now**

When you're finished, read what you wrote aloud.

One Imaginative Storm participant wrote about going up in a hot-air balloon and expecting the wind to be cold, then realizing that there was no wind because she was moving exactly as the air moved: she was at one with the air. Another wrote about running downhill, feeling like water cascading down the mountainside. Another wrote about a moment of terror when she lost her voice and felt only air inside her.

The James List: Irrepressible nature

The unexpected always has energy. When nature appears somewhere it's not "supposed" to be, there's a sense of a larger life happening beyond the immediate circumstances of the scene you're describing. It locates your story in a living universe.

Make a list of places where the presence of nature is unexpected. Interpret the word "nature" however you like.

Set your timer (5) **and make your list now**

Once you start observing all the unexpected ways the natural world interacts with human creation, you can see how this list could grow to include hundreds of combinations. Here are some examples from our workshops:

- *goat yoga*
- *mold behind sheetrock*
- *birds flying around inside a big box store*
- *whale breath in my camera*
- *7-foot cobra wrapped in my sleeping pad*

Think of all the effort humans expend to keep nature out. You probably try to keep bugs and mice out of your house. Scientists try to keep every scrap of organic matter out of sterile labs. And then one little virus particle gets in—and you've got a story.

Since everything in the universe is constantly changing, reforming, remaking itself, the possibilities are infinite. Now, let's consider the forces that make those changes happen.

Prompt: The forces that made it

Like "I don't remember" and "what wasn't there," this prompt asks you to write about a place from a perspective outside your usual awareness. When you write about the forces that made a place, you'll depart from your usual way of thinking about this place. Once again, you'll be writing what you don't know.

For example, when you think about what makes a backyard vegetable garden, you might think of soil, compost, sun, rain, seeds, you and your shovel. You might not think about the vitamin D in the sunlight, the person who packaged the seeds, the rainwater sinking into ancient aquifers, or the first human to think of planting things rather than foraging for them.

Our ordinary field of perception is so narrow we might as well be wearing blinders. It's exciting to realize how much there is behind, beneath, and beyond what we see every day.

Now, think about a place in nature that you feel a personal connection with, and write about the forces that made it. Just like the word "nature," feel free to interpret "the forces that made it" however you please. Go back to your younger self, your great-grandfather, or the Big Bang.

Set your timer (10) **and write now**

When you're finished, read what you wrote aloud.

One Imaginative Storm participant wrote about his father's workshop. (You might think he didn't follow the prompt exactly since a workshop isn't a place in nature, but to him it was, as it was surrounded by wooded countryside.) His father worked for the power company, and he followed his imagination as it took him to the memory of working-class men in hard hats. He'd put a turtle crossing the interstate on his James List of places where nature is unexpected, and that turtle made its way into this piece. He thought it was random, but when he read what he'd written aloud, we all saw the connection: the men were just like the turtle, wearing shells that might not be enough to protect them, trying to make their way through life with the threat of bigger forces squashing them flat.

The connection was so effortless that the writer didn't even realize it was there. That's the magic of reading aloud and having listeners: you notice things and they notice things.

When you approach what you know or remember from a new

perspective, you give your imagination the opportunity to pop out these powerful symbolic images. They feel organic; they have emotional resonance. When you make your rational mind do the work, the connections may come, but they often feel forced. But here's another thing: even if you did come up with the image in this organic way, if you did that a while ago you may have revisited it in your mind a few times and now, because of that familiarity, it may have become a little stale. In other words, it's now something you know—so when you write it on the page, it has that secondhand, half-alive feeling. So, we encourage you always to give your imagination opportunities to generate new connections, new images, new metaphors, new symbols.

We can't promise that something fresh and insightful will come out of your pen every time you write for 10 minutes. You never know when that will happen. But when you train regularly, you can be sure that it will come—and it will come more often and more easily if you let your imagination take the lead than if you try to force it to come with struggle and toil.

Surf the Storm

Prompt: Metaphorical elements

In this prompt, you'll use the elements again, this time in a deliberately metaphorical way.

Here are the six elements again:

earth   air   fire   water   wood   metal

You could also use an element from the periodic table, such as iron, or helium, or sulfur.

Now, choose one of the following phrases and fill in the gap with whatever element you like:

It was the year of _____   *It was the journey of* _____
It was the party of _____   *It was the city of* _____
It was the house of _____   *It was the marriage of* _____
It was the church of _____   *It was the dead end of* _____

Set your timer  **and write**

When you're finished, read what you wrote aloud.

Write with Curiosity

When you write what you don't know, you become curious about what will emerge. You've already seen how often you can surprise yourself in just 10 minutes of writing. You've probably had some personal insights by now, seen connections among the threads of your life that you'd never noticed, heard a confident, authentic voice you didn't know you had.

What might emerge in the next 10 minutes, 10 days, 10 years?

We are all naturally curious creatures. But we're not always taught to value our curiosity. You might even have had a parent who actively discouraged it—perhaps because they felt inadequate when they were unable to answer your childish questions. Remember that phase when you used to ask "Why?" about everything, and every answer led to a new "Why?" And eventually the adult you were interrogating just gave up—maybe amused, maybe frustrated or irritated or even angry?

When you write in the Imaginative Storm, you discover, or rediscover, the delight of curiosity. You feel how curiosity energizes you and motivates you. When you're curious about what you're writing, you're not stuck in writerly angst, obsessing over questions like "Can I do this? Am I a good writer? Will I ever be a good writer? Who cares what I write?" You're curious, so *you* care what you write—and that's all you need.

Doubt conjures fear. When you let those questions gnaw at you, what they're eating away is your creativity. The antidote is curiosity. It's there in you! Now, appreciate it. Nourish it. Follow it. Be curious about where your creativity will take you.

Have you ever doubted that you're a creative person? Maybe your house and clothes don't look arty. You don't play an instrument. You can't draw something that looks the way you want it to. We would say that those are just skills and inclinations that our culture labels "creative." They are no more than particular manifestations of something that we all share as the essence of what makes us human.

We are all naturally creative creatures, just as we are all naturally curious creatures. Creativity, like curiosity, is a species imperative.

We define creativity as the human desire to make form from the abundance of physical and experiential material around us. We humans are constantly organizing, constantly arranging things and thoughts in patterns that please us.

You're creative every time you look at something: like a visual artist, you've just decided on foreground and background. When you were a baby, you took in a massive amount of knowledge about the world—gravity, weather, what's hard and soft, what's hot and cold, and so on—and you started deciding what you liked, what excited you, what gave you pleasure. As an adult, you're creative when you decorate your house (even if you choose plain white tiles), when you arrange your dishes in the cabinets, when you play with a child, when you tell the story of the amazing thing that happened to you— which just happens to fall into a beginning, middle, and punch line. When you sing in the shower, the sound waves you create in the air carry rhythm and give you pleasure.

Conscious creativity is simply an extension of the unconscious creativity you were born with. You wonder what it will look like, or sound like, or smell like, or how it will work, or how it will make you (or someone else) feel, if you put elements together in a way they've never been put together before—so you try it. You try this combination and that combination. You're curious about what pattern will manifest that germ of an idea that suddenly appeared in your imagination.

The idea itself is just the spark. It comes out of "nowhere"—but really, it comes from letting your imagination play with possibilities and letting your rational mind be open to considering those possibilities. Curiosity is the oxygen that makes the fire of creativity catch.

When you create in this way, motivated and energized by curiosity, the subject matter doesn't have to be what people call "art." Maybe you design a new sales strategy for your business or a new set play for your soccer team.

Notice that when you accept this broad, generous perspective, your doubts about your own creativity naturally start to shrink. If you've ever doubted your creativity, now's the time to label that a mood, not a fact.

Using your creativity, you make order, and new order, from the abundance of mental and sensory information that bombards you daily. When you make sense of things, you feel more secure, more in control of your own experience of life. When you find new patterns and new orderings, your sense of engagement grows and you're curious to discover more, and more. Your rational mind and your imagination are partners in this exploration. That's why you, like all human beings on the planet, are drawn to stories—because at heart we're all curious about what makes us tick, and how to make sense of living in this universe of infinite connections and meanings and possibilities.

The expression of your creativity is your right, whether you're recognized for it or not. When you own it, you claim the validity and value of your perceptions of the world. You feel the baby's sense of security and pleasure in making order out of the welter of experience. Or, to be more grown-up, you could think of it as sitting beside the river of life and seeing patterns in its swirls.

Still, you've probably had times of feeling uncreative. You lacked inspiration. Nothing demanded that you make sense of it or explore it. Your imagination got frustrated and pulled in, which means you stopped noticing the little things that might inspire you: an overheard remark, a strange combination of objects or events, an intriguing situation that could have many outcomes. When you feel uncreative, it's because you're not delighting in the possibility of finding patterns in the smorgasbord of experience. Why?

One possibility is boredom. You might be a little bored with your current way of ordering experience, and the whole idea of experimenting with other ways feels boring by extension. You can't be bothered to explore. You've gotten stuck in what you know, so everything feels predictable.

Another possibility is overwhelm. With all that abundance, where do you even start?

A third possibility is fear. If life feels chaotic and threatening, you're not curious to explore it. Plus, everyone fears change to some extent, because the unknown carries an element of danger. When you create new patterns and forms from your experience, you're challenging the old ones. In other words, you're questioning what you know.

Curiosity is the starting point for doubt-free conscious creativity. That's what prompts are for! They encourage your imagination to go places it hasn't been before, and when you give it a safe environment in which to do so, you'll feel that urge to make pattern and order and connection quickly returning. (We'll discuss safety in more detail later on.) You'll notice again the things you love, the things that give you pleasure and intrigue you, and they will motivate you.

Tease your curiosity. Cajole your creativity. Creativity is the imagination having fun—and the more fun you have, the more you'll want to have.

In the imagination, as in the dream world, everything is possible. You probably couldn't stop your imagination picturing that zebra on a trapeze, chomping away on a pineapple. As Hamlet says to Horatio, "There are more things in heaven and earth than are dreamt of in your philosophy." As a writer working creatively, you're training your curiosity onto things as yet undreamt-of, along with all the other fascinating denizens of the kaleidoscope of your mind.

"If you're alive, you're a creative person. You and I and everyone you know are descended from tens of thousands of years of makers. Decorators, tinkerers, storytellers, dancers, explorers, fiddlers, drummers, builders, growers, problem-solvers, and embellishers—these are our common ancestors. The guardians of high culture will try to convince you that the arts belong only to a chosen few, but they are wrong and they are also annoying. . . . Your very body and your very being are perfectly designed to live in collaboration with inspiration, and inspiration is still trying to find you—the same way it hunted down your ancestors."

— Elizabeth Gilbert, *Big Magic*

Session 6:
Socialese

In the previous session, you explored the interconnectedness of the natural world. In this session, you'll explore the interconnectedness of the human part of it.

So, what's Socialese? It's a word we made up to describe the wordless language we all use to communicate. Whenever humans come together, gestures, expressions, body language, customs, and rituals are far more powerful means of communication than words. You can probably list a few elements of Socialese that are common to most people on the planet: a warm smile expressing welcome, an open hand showing there's no threat, a glare that means "stay away." But most Socialese is far more nuanced. Often it's specific to whatever subset of humanity uses it: men or women, cultures or families, professionals or hobbyists, and so on.

You may speak a dialect of Socialese with your cat or your dog. And if you meet a bear in the woods, it's good to know a few gestures of Bear Socialese so you'll know what to do.

Can you lie in Socialese? Well, people try all the time. Actors are very good at it, which is why they get the big bucks. But body language gives most people away, so it's easier to think of people who try to lie in Socialese but don't really get away with it. For example, that person who throws his arm around you and leans close to your face for a photo—is he really your best friend?

Because humans are such tribal creatures, Socialese has zillions of dialects. A dictionary of Socialese would be as extensive as the world. As far as such a dictionary exists, it exists in the pages of stories.

Seed the Storm

Prompt: Eating together

This warm-up is a simple one. Make a list of foods. Any foods, whatever springs to mind.

Set your timer (2) **and make your list now**

Did some of the foods that sprang to your mind surprise you—maybe because you're a vegetarian and a bacon cheeseburger popped up? Did people and circumstances come to mind alongside the food?

Many people say that every single food on their list is connected with a person or group of people. Look over your own list and think about those human connections. Make notes on your list if you like. Then choose one food from your list and write about the human connection that particular food represents in your life.

Set your timer **5** **and write now**

When you're finished, read what you wrote aloud.

The connections made by food are literally visceral. Maybe because food represents life, it's an important vector of the connections we make with one another. It carries cultural identity. It lubricates social situations. And it can represent an emotional connection in a way that's much more powerful than words.

You could call food a major dialect of Socialese.

Prompt: Initiation into a tribe

Unless you're a total hermit, you've been a member of many tribes in the course of your life. (There could, in theory, even be a tribe of hermits.) Here are some possibilities:

- family
- circles of friends
- workplace
- church
- town or neighborhood
- people you went to school or took a course with
- people you share a hobby with
- sports team
- fans of a sports team
- lifestyle warriors

Make a list of tribes you've belonged to over the years. Keep in mind that you don't have to know your fellow tribe members. For example, birders consider themselves part of the birdwatching tribe even though they may do their birdwatching in parties of one.

Set your timer **2** **and make your list now**

Being accepted into a tribe is a decisive moment: you were on the outside, and now you're on the inside. Fraternities are notorious for their initiation rites, but not all initiation rites are so extreme or obvious. For other tribes, being accepted is more a matter of accomplishing something or reaching a milestone. Or perhaps it's just a subtle personal change—a shift in your thinking, a change in your behavior—and you realize you belong.

Some tribes accept anyone who wants to join. Others are very choosy. With the choosy ones, you may never be quite sure if you're in yet.

Now, pick one of the tribes on your list and ask yourself: What was my initiation?

Set your timer **10** **and write now**

When you're finished, read what you wrote aloud.

As you look back over your list of tribes you've belonged to, think about which ones overlap and which ones contradict. When you joined one tribe, did that mean you were 86'd from another one? Did you manage to balance your membership in two tribes simultaneously—such as the nerds and the cool kids? You might have been tugged in different directions, tugged between opposing loyalties.

Loyalty is another very powerful human motivation, because we all want to belong and we want to be seen to be belonging.

So here's another opportunity to put a contradiction, an opposition, into your story.

The James List: Social customs you love

You've likely enjoyed the camaraderie of many tribes in the course of your life. If you've ever been to a class reunion, you've noticed how people fall back into familiar customs and rituals, no matter how many years have passed.

These customs and rituals are not just markers of who's in and who's out. They're carrying the emotional connection and the identity of that group. Then there are other social customs that just punctuate your day: pleasantries, grace notes in life. These customs develop naturally, and they become precious.

Make a list of social customs you love.

Set your timer 5 and make your list now

There's something nourishing about simply recognizing customs like these. They're the visible bonds of human connection. Always, when we do this prompt in a group and read our lists aloud, people exclaim enthusiastically, "Me too!" So here are some examples of customs treasured by Imaginative Storm participants which might have resonance for you:

- *the French greeting of a kiss on each cheek*
- *roadside crosses decorated with plastic flowers marking the place where someone died*
- *holding the door for a stranger*
- *dressing up for church*
- *the way parents at a school recital all say, "Hey, that's my kid"*
- *the way you hail a taxi in Cairo*
- *dancing with Dad to Christmas carols*
- *how long-haul truckers flash their lights to say "thank you" when you let them pass*
- *the male nod: two men nod from a distance to convey "we're passing in peace"*

Even if it's not a custom you personally relate to (maybe Christmas carols were your negative rant in Session 2), the mere fact that someone loves a custom makes it precious. And if you've never hailed a taxi in Cairo, you're probably now curious about how it's done.

Prompt: A defining word or catchphrase

Many groups of people have a catchphrase, or can be seen through the lens of a word or a concept. For example, here in Taos, New Mexico, people are always saying, "It's Taos!" When something wonderful happens: "It's Taos!" Something awful: "It's Taos." Something downright bizarre: "Hey, it's Taos . . ."

One Imaginative Storm participant wrote about how people in Wisconsin say "hey" in virtually every sentence. A woman who had worked as a crew member on a billionaire's yacht wrote a brilliant piece with the refrain "We can do it!" A shih-tzu puppy before noon? "We can do it!" Pizza at 3 a.m. in the middle of the Mediterranean? "We can do it!" Probably they didn't actually say those words; this is what we mean by a concept that describes a group. Other possibilities might be something like "hierarchy" or "loosey-goosey" or "dog-eat-dog."

Phrases like those are markers of a group, but they don't exclude. Other phrases, like code words, might be markers of who's in and who's out. For example, during the Second World War, the British were told to say "silly mid off" to strangers. If the stranger didn't know what that meant he was almost certainly a German spy, since Germans don't play cricket. And some phrases have judgment baked into them. Here's another British example: "stiff upper lip." Is a stiff upper lip better than a wobbly, emotional lip? What does that say about the stiff-upper-lip tribe?

For this prompt, you'll write about a tribe or a social group, using a catchphrase, or a word, that expresses its identity. You might like to look back over your list of tribes. Do any of them have a catchphrase or a concept that defines them?

Set your timer (10) and write now

When you're finished, read what you wrote aloud.

Did you experience a sense of belonging, or maybe a sense of entrapment, while writing to this prompt? Belonging is an incredibly powerful human motivation. Characters in your writing, whether real or fictional, are constantly negotiating their position in regard to various groups they're part of, or want to be part of, or wish they could escape from.

Surf the Storm

Prompt: The rules

Rules—written and unwritten—order our lives. We all have to navigate the tension between what's allowed and what's not allowed, and every group of people has things that are okay and things that are not okay. For example, in certain cultures, it's considered rude to belch after you eat, while in others, it's rude not to. It's not just manners that vary; moral rules vary too. Just think of the Mafia.

Some rules you respect. Others you despise. Some rules are imposed on you. Some you make for yourself. Some rules restrict, oppress, or mislead. Some you have to discover, such as how to drive in Manila or how to offer a bribe.

Some rules provide a useful framework, as when you're writing a screenplay, or present a fun challenge—have you ever tried to write a haiku or a villanelle? Many rules are actually a comfort.

Think about times in your life when you had to deal with rules. You might want to make a list.

When you're ready to write, choose a time when rules of some kind dominated the situation, and start with this sentence, filling in the middle with whichever word you like:

That was when I

broke
massaged
rewrote
jettisoned
invented
shattered
made fun of

the rules.

What did you do? And, what desire or need prompted you to do it?

Set your timer  and write

When you're finished, read what you wrote aloud.

Write Without Attachment

You've probably seen a writer in a movie yanking the paper out of the typewriter and throwing it at the trash can, and it misses and lands on the floor among lots of other balled-up pieces of paper. We are supposed to think this is a frustrated writer whose work is not going well.

But what if the writing is going well? What if throwaway writing is a vital part of the creative process?

Photographers shoot a thousand images and throw away the vast majority of them. Artists draw in sketchbooks—thousands of pictures that will never be seen by the public. Musicians noodle around with chords, not knowing if they'll turn into a melody or not. This is all "throwaway" work. And it's essential.

But, like many people, you may have bought into the idea that this doesn't apply to writers. You may have thought that your writing was supposed to come out more or less "right" the first time. You know the language, so why did the words not add up to what you want to say? You might have thought that the fault is with you: you're just not talented enough. You're not "a good writer."

So, what's a good writer? What's "good writing"?

Because good writing takes so many shapes and forms, let's just say that good writing is writing that feels good to you. It feels like your voice, saying what you want to say. It has verve. It has the tang of truth.

You may have a concept of "good writing" that goes beyond that—the work of writers you admire, a style of writing you aspire to. That's fine. Just know that those writers may well not have written that way when they first started throwing words onto the page. Also, they weren't "trying" to write in a certain style. They were just trying to express themselves, or tell a story, in the most powerful way they could—and letting their style grow from the way their material was filtered and interpreted and embroidered and distilled by their imagination.

So, do what they did. Focus on the process, not the result.

That's why the Writer Training is built around 10-minute bursts of writing. Before you began using our prompts, you probably believed it's impossible to come up with "good writing" in 10 minutes. By now, you may have changed your mind. We frequently hear people say that they wrote better in 10 minutes than they're used to doing in an hour, or even all day, which is a rather amazing reversal. (More on reversals in Session 10.) Why would this be?

We all do many things in life because we want a particular result. It's natural to focus on that result, to want it to come quickly, to want there to be a clear path leading directly to it from where you are now. Unfortunately, this mindset isn't helpful for writing. As soon as you start thinking about the result, you start assessing whether you're getting closer to it or further from it. Or whether you're getting closer to it fast enough. Or whether you'll ever reach it at all. This is why an indefinite writing period, or even a longer timer such as 20 or 30 minutes, can be problematic: it gives you time to fixate on the result. But 10 minutes is throwaway. If you get nothing of interest at all—which is unlikely, though possible—big deal. You only spent 10 minutes.

You can spend 10 minutes and 10 minutes and 10 minutes—but each 10 minutes is throwaway. Like photographers and musicians and artists, you're doing "throwaway" work which serves a vital purpose: honing your skills, letting your imagination play, giving yourself material to work with.

Almost certainly, you won't throw all of it away. You'll find gems in this material, and perhaps you'll decide to set them and polish them. The thing is, you can't identify the gems until after you've done the writing, just like the photographer, clicking away, doesn't know which shots will make the final cut. Statistically, each shot is very likely to be thrown away.

When you embrace the idea of throwaway writing, you stop trying and just write. You take pleasure in stringing words together the way a musician takes pleasure in the sounds of the notes. Your imagination feels appreciated and gets jazzed up, since it knows that your inner critic isn't going to slap it down by saying "That's not good enough" or "That's stupid" or "That's not relevant to my project." Your imagination doesn't give you gifts if it thinks they're going to be rejected.

If you're a task-oriented person, this may be a challenge for you. You want to feel that every expenditure of time and energy brings you closer to completing the task—so you may need to reframe your idea of what the task is. Do you want to just get something finished, or do you want to make it as good as it can possibly be, by expanding your range and power as a writer?

There may be some lucky folks who create in the mythical flow that the poor movie writer is failing to reach, but most writers will tell you that's not how it works at all. Most of what they write is exploration and experiment. They don't start at the beginning, because they don't know where the beginning is. They write exponentially more material than ever lands on the published page.

The screenwriting guru Robert McKee calls this "research." When you write to Imaginative Storm prompts, you're researching into your imagination and your philosophy of life, your experiences and your judgments of them. You're revisiting parts of your life and areas of your thinking from new perspectives. You're getting insights into people, places, and story.

So, if you're attached to an idea of what a writer is "supposed" to be, here's your opportunity to give it up! You don't have to call yourself an "aspiring writer" or a "fledgling writer." You don't have to "find your voice" or have "writer's block" or other writerly problems to be part of the writer tribe.

You're writing as you do this Writer Training. That makes you a writer.

Nothing you put onto a blank page has to be "good." It doesn't have to be grammatical or correctly spelled. It doesn't have to be coherent. It doesn't have to make rational sense. The editing stage comes later. Give yourself permission to throw the bulk of what you write away—without attachment. Let's say 10% of what you write is final draft material—which is a pretty fantastic ratio. You still have to write the other 90%.

And even if you never use a word of Imaginative Storm material in your "real" writing, it has other uses. Exploring your life and your perceptions expands your view of yourself and the world around you. The expansion stays with you forever.

"I write a lot of material that I know I'll throw away. It's just part of the process. I have to write hundreds of pages before I get to page one."

— Barbara Kingsolver, on her writing
process, "The Office" online

Session 7:
Tender Spots

In the previous session, "Socialese," you explored patterns of unspoken communication. Those rules and manners developed, in part, to help us get along with one another—to avoid misunderstandings and missteps. They smooth out the surface of human interaction. But beneath the surface, things aren't smooth at all.

You may have heard someone described as a "spiky" character. They're touchy, quick to anger. In fact, we are all spiky in our own way—even people who seem to be soft and yielding. Because spikes also face inward.

Those spikes hit the tender spots: weaknesses, vulnerabilities, fears, doubts, disappointments, resentments, deprivations. Each person's combination is unique; that's what makes us individuals. Our failings and frustrations define who we are, maybe even more than our hopes and desires do. Tolstoy begins his novel *Anna Karenina* with the observation, "All happy families are alike. Each unhappy family is unhappy in its own way." That goes for people, too. Most of us want "happiness"—but we define it according to the lacks and pains and sorrows we feel.

In the language of Socialese, it's considered rude to point out someone's trigger points. But politeness doesn't help you as a writer. That's why we encouraged you to rant.

So, don't be "polite" as you delve into character in this session. Everybody guards their tender spots. The writer's job is to see both the armor *and* what's beneath it. As you work with character, there's a pivot between being freely creative and being almost forensic—and you'll do both in this session. You'll be playful with the messages that people send out to their fellow speakers of Socialese, and you'll go inside, to discover how to find, and compassionately portray, the tender spots.

Vulnerability creates intimacy. When you see someone else's frailty—in life, or on the page—it makes your mirror neurons fire, because you too have frailties that you try to hide. You and that person, real or fictional, become allies in the difficult task of living life. If you're writing about a real person—say, in a memoir—look for moments when they revealed their vulnerability to you. If you're creating a fictional character, you'll need to discover what haunts them and what triggers them.

Most of us feel a gap between who we are and who we think we're supposed to be. Maybe your sister loves compliments, but you—due to some particular ideas about yourself, however they got there—feel squirrelly at being the center of attention. Maybe you know someone who tenses up when his father, or professional success, is the subject of the conversation—what fears or doubts or resentments is he trying to suppress? One person boasts about overcoming a deprived childhood; another does everything possible to make sure nobody knows. Or perhaps you're an introvert but your society rewards extroverts: how do you behave? By retreating, or overcompensating?

If you know a person's history, you might think that a particular life experience "explains" a sensitivity, but it's not cause-and-effect. It's why the scar is there, but it doesn't explain the shape of the scar. The child of an alcoholic might become an alcoholic themselves, or a bartender, or a Buddhist, or a mercenary, or anything else under the sun. The scars of life shape personality, but people deal with those scars in wildly different ways.

That's what makes human nature so fascinating, and so baffling. What strange creatures we are. What strange things we do—and what's driving us to do them? How do we each find a way of making sense of our experience of the world?

Human nature is not a recipe. You don't put certain ingredients into a child, bake for a decade or two, and know what kind of person will result. Equally, it doesn't work to try and reverse-engineer a character by finding some childhood trauma that "explains" who they are. So, when you're putting a character on the page, you don't need to tell your reader precisely why their tender spots are tender, just as in real life you don't necessarily know why, exactly, people are sensitive in the way they are. All you need to do, to make a character feel real, is give your reader a sense of the psychological undercurrents swirling beneath the character's words and actions.

When someone's tender spots are touched, they're motivated to take action of some kind: maybe to hide or overcome a failing; to turn away from something they can't bear to face; to achieve, or give up on, some longed-for goal. So, when you understand the tender spots of the characters you're writing about, you have a sense of what situations will press on them and reveal them. This is how you make character drive story.

Seed the Storm

Prompt: Dressing up

Clothing, like food, carries much more meaning than just its basic purpose. It sends messages. It expresses mood. When someone dresses in order to feel like the person they wish they were, or in order to make a certain impression, their clothing betrays a tender spot.

For this warm-up, make a list of articles of clothing: eccentric, outlandish, or something so ordinary that you might never even think about it.

Set your timer **2** **and make your list now**

Here are some articles of clothing that other Imaginative Storm participants put on their lists. Add any of them to your own list if you like.

burqa	*bustle*	*velociraptor heels*
boratkini	*hair shirt*	*onesie*
priest's collar	*brass skull ring*	*toe socks*
jeggings	*black du-rag*	*"Viva Mexico!" sombrero*
paper dress	*dad hat*	*Mardi Gras mask*

Now—before you read on—choose five articles of clothing from your list and circle them.

Okay, you've got five randomly assorted articles of clothing. For the writing part of this prompt, imagine a person, real or fictional, wearing all five of those articles of clothing—at the same time. Why would they do that?

Set your timer **5** **and write now**

When you're finished, read what you wrote aloud.

How weird was the character you wrote about? Some of the characters that emerge from this prompt are more believable than others—but they all have some level of believability. We think that's because there's intention baked into this. They did put on all five of those articles of clothing for some reason; or, if they've found themselves so oddly dressed, some storyline has put them in that place and they're responding in a certain way—trying to get them off, or pretending it's all entirely normal.

You'd probably never put all five of those articles of clothing on a character in your "serious" writing. But maybe one of them is a perfect signifier for something you want to convey, and you might never have thought of it if you weren't walking on the weird side. Weird has energy. It's good to develop a sense of freedom around being weird.

Even very ordinary items of clothing can generate a spark, when you focus on them. One participant wrote about going on a hike and feeling the wet, sweaty T-shirt sticking to his back—a detail he might not have thought of if the T-shirt hadn't been sitting there on his list, waiting to be used.

And did you notice the value of being specific? "Sneakers" doesn't say much, but "Converse Chuck Taylors" or "immaculate vintage Nikes" carry lots of messages. Question those messages! They may be very different from what the character intended when they got dressed.

Prompt: An unattractive physical characteristic

What came to mind when you read those words: "an unattractive physical characteristic"? Did you think of something like a hunchback, or rotting teeth, or an ugly birthmark?

Those words might even have made you feel a little uncomfortable; many people don't like to think they're being unkind. But unattractive is a subjective judgment, not an objective fact. What one person thinks is unattractive, another may find beautiful. The harshest critic is often the person who's looking in the mirror. You probably know someone who's drop-dead gorgeous but obsessed with a minuscule flaw.

Physical appearance is a tender spot for many people, and they protect it in different ways. For this prompt, you'll describe a person, real or fictional, starting from an unattractive physical characteristic. Define "unattractive" however you wish.

Set your timer **10** **and write now**

When you're finished, read what you wrote aloud.

How far did you stretch the meaning of "unattractive"? In fact, you could write about a very beautiful person in response to this prompt, because that kind of beauty can be intimidating. Instead of attracting, it repels. The beautiful person walks into a room, and nobody dares to go near them.

This is the prompt we set long ago in Ireland that spurred the rant about ears poking through long straight hair. Another memorable example was a woman who began with the sentence, "My mother always said I had a thick waist." What a fantastic opening line! An immediate insight into an intense and difficult relationship, and—because of the unresolved conflict the sentence expresses—a suggestion of story ready to unfold.

If you wrote about someone you know, you may have felt uncomfortable being uncomplimentary or blunt. Notice what constraining yourself felt like—and what it felt like to break through the constraint. Prompts which invite you to "say the wrong thing" are retraining your inner critic. You're teaching it that the standard it needs to uphold here is not good manners or keeping your nose out of other people's business, but creative courage. Are you letting your imagination take the lead? Are you being absolutely honest? Are you stretching the boundaries of your compassion? Are you willing to explore into awkward, even upsetting territory?

Another demon you may have faced in writing to this prompt is that when you come from a "negative" perspective, you find the negative in yourself. Maybe, as you wrote, you felt ashamed of yourself for being unkind or intrusive or so observantly petty. Or maybe you felt a bit high on the glee of being malicious—and experienced the interesting struggle between what we actually think and what we think we're supposed to think (or not think).

Don't worry: what you write in this Training never needs to leave your notebook. But you might decide to use what you wrote for a fictional character who isn't identifiable as the person you know. Still, even if you never use it again, it's possible that what you wrote gave you insight into what it's like to be the innocent provoker of other people's guilty discomfort.

The James List: Soothing tender spots

This James List is a little different from the previous ones, which were on the warm and fuzzy side. Like the last prompt, this one may make you feel a little uncomfortable. If so, keep in mind what we said above: this is good information! You're learning what's been constraining you as a writer. It will also pique your curiosity. Why does this particular reality make you uncomfortable?

Start by thinking about yourself and your own tender spots. What do you do to soothe yourself when nobody is watching?

Now think about people you know and what they may do when nobody is watching. What tender spots might they be soothing? What feelings or judgments about themselves would they not want anyone to know? Keep this in list form rather than joined-up writing.

Set your timer (10) and make your list

Scenes like these are powerful in your writing because you're showing someone at their most vulnerable. You're revealing a secret moment that, in reality, the person would never allow another human being to see.

When you wrote about people you know, you may have felt you were intruding. But you're not claiming that your speculations are correct; you're just entertaining possibilities in the hope of gaining understanding, which is a worthy goal. If you write about those people in a memoir, or create a fictional character, this exercise will have given you a way to suggest their tender spots. This intrusive, impolite probing is a compassionate act.

Prompt: Empathy with a villain

First of all, what's a villain? Maybe the word brings up a mental image of a mustache-twirling criminal chuckling sadistically. Have you ever met anyone like that, for real? Probably not. But you have villains in your life. People who were cruel to you, obstructed you, or harmed you physically or mentally.

It can be difficult to portray an unpleasant character without making them seem one-dimensional, a stock villain. To make them real on the page, you have to find empathy—in other words, awareness of your shared humanity.

By empathy, we don't mean sympathy. You don't have to excuse or justify the person, you don't have to forgive them, you don't have to like them, you don't have to feel sorry for them. What you do have to do is recognize that they're human and they have tender spots, and that the behavior that hurt you is, in some way, the expression of how they are responding to a tender spot.

If you're tempted to create an imaginary character for this prompt, resist the temptation! But notice it: again, this is good information for what may have been constraining you as a writer. Choose someone you genuinely feel did you wrong, and consider two questions:

- What were they afraid of?
  Not a phobia, like spiders or heights. What, in their deepest selves, might they have been afraid of?
- What had they lost?

Set your timer (10) **and write now**

When you're finished, read what you wrote aloud.

Asking what someone is afraid of, or what someone has lost, is an excellent way to locate a tender spot. When you turn your awareness away from their actions to what might be driving those actions, you open a window of empathy. You don't have to understand exactly why the particular actions were their response to a tender spot being pressed. It's enough to know there's a tender spot there, and to give some suggestion of what it might be.

Most people are not actually trying to be villainous. Usually, people are trying to do the best they can in the circumstances they find themselves in, even though the best they can do might be less than a 1 on your scale of 1 to 10. And even those people who we would all agree are world-class villains don't see themselves as villains at all.

So, if you're trying to make a "villain" character more real on the page, you don't have to give them some likeable characteristic, such as being kind to animals. Although, imagine what tender spot that Bond villain might be soothing as he strokes his cat.

Surf the Storm

Prompt: Animal avatars

If you had to pick an animal that characterizes you, what animal would you choose? Do you zip across the room like a squirrel, or lumber like a hippopotamus? Do you attack fiercely like a mountain lion, or lie in wait like a leopard? Do you like to travel great distances like a caribou, or do you prefer to stay close to home like a prairie dog? Do you put your head down and work till you're done like a mule, or do you gaze around and take in the scenery like a zebra?

Maybe zebras don't actually do that, but you might feel they do. Especially if that's you and you like stripes.

Working with an animal image to develop a character is a basic actor's exercise. In developing his character in *The Godfather*, Marlon

Brando landed on the image of a bulldog with a bullet in its throat. When the brilliant stage actor Antony Sher played Shakespeare's Richard III, he made drawings to help him find his animal image. They're included in his book *The Year of the King*. Richard III was a hunchback. What animal has a hunchback shape? A bull. That didn't do it for him. What happens if you have a hunchback? You're bent over, so you might want short canes to help you walk. When Sher drew that and the shadow it cast, he saw a spider.

A great example of this in fiction is in John Banville's novel *The Untouchable*, where he describes a Middle European prince as being like an old, battle-scarred crocodile. There's a wonderful detail of this man, with a large head and barrel chest, balancing on two little feet like a stuffed-animal crocodile. (Banville doesn't say that specifically—we're just guessing that's where he got the image.) When the man is introduced, he's friendly, but everybody knows you shouldn't trust a crocodile.

In one of our workshops for the screenwriting students at the National University of Ireland, Galway, two people compared someone to a lion. One, who was Irish, used the standard characteristics: proud, majestic, dominating. The other, who was from Zimbabwe, knew more about lions. The character he wrote about was like a lion because he was lazy and scruffy and let the women do all the work.

Start by making a list of people who remind you of animals, and make a note of the shared characteristic that brings the animal to mind.

Choose one pairing that intrigues you, and research the animal. Watch a nature documentary. Go to the zoo or a farm. Look for other qualities that the animal and the person share.

You'll probably learn some new things about the animal. What kind of noise does it make? What's its social life? How long does it live, and in what environments? What does it eat?

You might want to do this prompt for multiple characters, as research. Later, when you come to edit, you might decide to remove any mention of the animal, just as actors don't provide liner notes

on their prep. A few animal-specific words—or maybe just one—
will give your character that bite.

Set your timer  **and write**

When you're finished, read what you wrote aloud.

Write Without Censorship

You might write something that unsettles you. Even as you're writing it you may be wondering what mean or sick or ungenerous part of your brain that came from. You might think, "It's not okay to think that, let alone write it down!" So you feel the urge to censor yourself.

Resist the urge! Don't censor yourself—not at this point, anyway. That material is true to you, in this moment. It's authentic. It's your voice. And it doesn't need to go anywhere beyond your notebook.

What kind of material might you be tempted to censor? Would you feel bad about:

- writing something critical of someone you know
- showing someone you love in an unflattering light
- showing yourself in an unflattering light
- telling a truth that someone else would prefer be kept secret
- depicting cruel actions, such as torture
- creating an "evil" character, such as Hannibal Lecter
- treating serious subject matter lightly or satirically
- writing about sex
- depicting the glamor of violence
- being critical of or rejecting religious strictures

If you want to write well, you have to be honest. That doesn't mean you have to spill your guts to the world or air all your family's dirty laundry. But your inclinations, morals, prejudices, and values will show—even if you're writing poetry or fiction. Your poem or story will mean something about the way human beings navigate the world.

And if it's not "you," what's the point of writing it? To make money, maybe? Truth is, any piece of writing that isn't authentic to the writer doesn't stand much chance of being a success.

We really like the advice given by a poet named Jack Myers on how to write poetry: you just wallow around in the swamp of your psychology until you find something to write about. What's wallowing? Just writing stuff, exploring, poking around. Exactly what you're doing in the Writer Training. And the swamp? Gunky and gooey, but also beautiful and alive with creatures—especially at night. Frogs, birds, fish, and mammals of many kinds. Plus, venomous snakes and alligators.

Everybody has alligators and snakes in the swamp of their psychology. Awful experiences you've lived through. Terrors, waking nightmares, cruel or ungenerous thoughts. A writer who pretends these things don't exist is sugar-coating life. Fears and fury have power, so treat them with care—but don't banish them from your writing.

You can be true to yourself and still allow for endless possibilities. Just because you see the world in a certain way, or have certain values, doesn't mean everyone else should agree. So just as you don't censor yourself, don't censor the worldviews or values of other characters—even if you don't agree with them. Let them have their say. You've probably heard it said that the villain has all the best lines (for example, "I'm having an old friend for dinner")—when that happens, there's an author who enjoyed letting the villain have his say.

If you're thinking crazy thoughts, does that mean you're close to madness? "Stop there!" says your rational mind. But beneath that, you can probably feel your imagination having fun pushing your boundaries—however uncomfortable it makes you. You might think, "That's not me. I am not the kind of person who thinks these things." But guess what? You are.

Thomas Harris, who wrote *The Silence of the Lambs*, accepted his dark imaginings, valued them, and explored them. Hannibal Lecter's actions are horrible—but frankly, nothing you can't find by looking through a few years of newspapers. There's probably at least one human being on the planet capable of doing anything that can be imagined.

You might want to do what Harris did and work your dark imaginings into a monstrous character. Or you might just shut that notebook for good and start a new one, or even rip out the page and burn it. But we hope you don't censor yourself after the fact either. Even if you do, your imagination won't forget what you wrote, because it's so powerfully out of your ordinary. The day may come when you realize your imagination has been noodling away at that frightening idea, and suddenly you're intrigued to see what you can make of it.

Letting the dark stuff come out is valuable in itself, because you're telling your imagination that it's allowed to stretch as far as it wants. But this is not to say that everything you write has to contain edgy material—only that if this material is part of your imaginative repertoire, allow that to happen. As soon as you start prescribing for yourself what you should and shouldn't write, self-consciousness and stiffness creep in.

"The creative act requires not only freedom but also this assumption of freedom. If the creative artist worries if he will still be free tomorrow, then he will not be free today. If he is afraid of the consequences of his choice of subject or of his manner of treatment of it, then his choices will not be determined by his talent, but by fear. If we are not confident of our freedom, then we are not free."

— Salman Rushdie, "On Censorship," *New Yorker*

Session 8:
Take Yourself Back

Throughout the Writer Training, we've encouraged you to mine your own life experience, since you are your best source of information about human nature, and human nature is at the heart of all compelling stories. In this session, we'll focus on memoir.

Even if you have no intention of writing a memoir, you'll find the prompts in this session intriguing and suggestive. You'll see yourself and the events of your life from perspectives that you may never have imagined. You'll become aware of the long-term impact of events you thought you'd left behind. You'll engage in 10-minute bursts of self-exploration that may make you feel challenged, uncomfortable, even shocked—but also curious and excited to discover more. And who knows, maybe you do have a memoir in your future!

You might think, "I'm not entitled to write a memoir—or, maybe I could write one, but who would read it? Why should anyone care what happened to me?" This question has been asked, with doubt and angst turned up to 10, and this was the answer, from a wise friend: people care about the characters in novels and they're not even real.

True, right?

Why? Because, as we explored in the previous session, you identify with anyone, real or fictional, who is dealing with the vicissitudes of life. Your mirror neurons fire as you recognize their yearnings and their fears. You search their lives for clues about how to understand and navigate your own. The author of a successful memoir doesn't have to be famous, just as nobody has ever heard of the protagonist of most novels before they begin reading.

We called this session "Take Yourself Back" for two reasons. When you're telling your own story, you take yourself back to times and places in your past. But you might also need to reclaim yourself from the judgments and expectations other people have put on you, and the judgments and expectations you've put on yourself. You've been encouraged to develop expectations—and they may not even accord with your innermost desires, your values, your needs. Most memoirs are, in the end, about self-realization. What self is yours to realize? Have you done that yet?

Often, when people start working on a memoir, they feel they already know the story, which is why they want to write it in the first place. But if you write entirely from your present-day perspective, the story feels inauthentic and rehearsed—because, in living your life, you don't know what will happen next, or what your experiences will eventually mean as you undergo them. You don't know how the story will turn out. So, in writing memoir, your challenge is to get yourself back into the present of your past—when you didn't know how the story was going to turn out, when you didn't know how any of these people and places and events would reverberate in your future.

Every second is a moment of arrival at what you don't know.

Seed the Storm

Prompt: Roles

Make a list of the roles you've played in your life. Some roles are practical, for example, parent, chauffeur, chef, nurse, mentor. Others are social and psychological, for example, problem-solver, victim, clown, truth-teller, therapist.

Set your timer (2) **and make your list now**

Now, think about the various roles you've played in your life, and ask yourself:

- Which suited me best?
- Which didn't suit me at all?
- Is there a role I'd like to play that I don't?
- Is there a role I'd like to play better?

Set your timer (5) **and write now**

When you're finished, read what you wrote aloud.

Did you feel the spark of insight when you made a discovery?

This story that you're living out may not be true to what you really love, what you really desire or hope to achieve, what you really care about in the world. So, as you explore further into your own story, you may discover that it's not quite what you thought it was before you began the Writer Training. You may be discovering a new sense of your personal journey.

Prompt: Take yourself back

Up to this point, you've been questioning your memory for both completeness and accuracy. Question your judgments, too—about yourself and about other people. As you generate the raw material for memoir, question everything.

Have you ever felt diminished, railroaded, or gaslighted by other people's judgments or expectations of you? Maybe you didn't even realize that the expectation or judgment wasn't your own, and you were trying to be who someone else wanted you to be. Have you ever felt like you lost yourself in a situation or a relationship? Have you ever felt like you were a supporting character in someone else's life rather than the central character in your own?

You can also reverse these questions. Have you ever railroaded or gaslighted somebody? Have you overwhelmed somebody else and forced them into a supporting role, even if you didn't intend to? Turning the questions on yourself will pry you away from your ready answers.

Think back over your life and identify times when you gave away your power or your sense of self. You might have had good intentions—say, you postponed a personal project to help a friend in need—but as time goes on, you lose yourself in somebody else's priorities and desires and ambitions at the expense of your own.

Start by making a short list of the times in your life when you gave yourself away. Be brutally honest. You don't have to show this list to anyone.

Set your timer (**3**) **and make your list now**

Now, choose one of those times when you gave yourself away, and ask yourself: Did I take myself back? Might I still need to?

Set your timer (**10**) **and write now**

When you're finished, read what you wrote aloud.

Most of us think of story in terms of "things" that happened: dramatic events, crises, milestones. You might think you're supposed to start work on a memoir by carving a story out of your life using those incidents as wayposts. You can tie yourself up in knots trying to create an outline, and likely you'll end up with one that makes rational sense. How do you feel when you look at it? Energized, or tired? If the answer is tired, then your outline isn't making imaginative sense.

The Imaginative Storm approach is to let your imagination tell you which events are important, rather than trying to figure it out rationally, by simply generating material around the story you want to tell. Your imagination is hooked into what makes you *you*, and it's far more interested in what you don't know than in what you do know. It doesn't care *what* happened to you. What it cares about is *what effect* it had on you—especially if you weren't aware of it at the time.

Prompts like this one invite your imagination to unearth the story of *you* beneath the story of the events that happened to you. That's the story people want to read. They don't care what happened to you. They care what you made of it, and what it made of you.

The James List: Times you were in the wrong

Nobody's perfect. We've all been in the wrong multiple times in our lives, in big ways and small. Make a list.

Different kinds of events may pop into your mind. Times when you were absolutely, definitely in the wrong; and other times when you didn't think you were in the wrong at all, but someone else thought you were. Times when you weren't really in the wrong, as you know now, but at the time you felt you were; and other times when you suspected correctly at the time that you were in the wrong, but later managed to convince yourself you were justified.

See if you can think of the very first time you felt you were in the wrong. You were a child—maybe three or four, twelve at most. You felt a burning shame, and as you think about it now, the burn lingers. Your memory may have buried the significance of the event because it burned so, or it may have been something you chastised yourself for, for years. Because there's only one answer to this question, it will come with a jolt. You might gasp or shout out a word or two that would be bleeped on the radio.

Take longer than usual for this James List.

Set your timer **10** **and write now**

As you made your list, you might have gotten a sudden insight into a time when you were in the wrong but until today, you thought that you weren't. You might expect that such a realization would come as an awful shock—and maybe you felt a bit of trepidation when you approached this prompt, thinking it would be an ordeal. But if you did get such an insight, was it unpleasant, or was it funny? Often insights come as funny, because you're amazed at how wrong—in a different sense—you can be.

Treasure that, when it happens. You have an authenticity check over your own memory. You now know what it feels like to accept a truth your rational mind has been trying to hide. And it's not that bad, is it? Might there be more?

Just making a list like this is a powerful way to take ownership of your mistakes and accept them with compassion rather than judgment. Whatever mistakes you made, you were doing the best you could with the tools and life experience you had available.

And, like all these prompts, you can do this one in the voices of your characters if you're writing fiction. What mistakes have those people made and how do they feel about them now? What do they regret? What are they trying to justify still, and maybe not entirely succeeding?

Prompt: The need that drives you

Desire, and need, are the engine of story. When somebody wants something, they take action to get it. When somebody needs something—let's say security, or family, or self-esteem—their need drives the way they respond to the circumstances that befall them.

That's what you'll work with in this prompt. Go back to the James List you just made and choose a time when you were definitely in the wrong. Now, ask yourself two questions:

- What did you want?
- What did you need?

You didn't do wrong for no reason. You didn't do wrong because you intended to do wrong. You did wrong because for some reason, you felt you had to. What desire, or need, was driving you?

Set your timer  and write now

When you're finished, read what you wrote aloud.

Did you feel any kind of release as you wrote to this prompt? In the past, you may have beaten yourself up over your wrong action, or you may have tried to justify it, or you may have managed to convince yourself that things happened a bit differently than how they really did. That's your rational mind at work, trying in various ways to make you a good person in your own eyes.

But when you approach the incident from the realm of "I don't know," your imagination is taking the lead, and it doesn't operate in the realm of moral judgment. It doesn't care whether you were wrong or right. It's far more interested in exploring why you did what you did.

You were driven by needs, the way everybody is. And sometimes they send you in a direction you regret. Think back to the "Empathy with a Villain" prompt in the previous session: has what you just wrote given you a little more insight into that person too?

Most memoirs—maybe all of them—have a happy ending, which is why people want to write them and why people love to read them. Almost always, they're stories of self-realization. So almost always, memoirs are driven by a need. Something is lacking—either because of a catastrophic event, or because the writer gradually becomes aware of the lack—and in the course of the story, the writer comes to terms with that need: either it's fulfilled, or the writer makes peace with it.

You have a primary need in your life, and that's the spine of the story you'll tell. You may still be in the process of discovering it.

So, think back to other times in your life when you did something unexpected, or dangerous, or rebellious. Think back to the "Surf the Storm" prompt of Session 6, "Socialese," about the rules: what need was driving you when you rewrote or massaged or jettisoned the rules? Think back to what you wrote about this session: a time when you gave yourself away, when you did what was asked or expected of you, or what you thought was expected of you, at some cost to yourself. What need was driving you then?

Surf the Storm

Prompt: Your own tender spots

In Session 7, you explored how tender spots bring characters alive on the page. If you're writing a memoir, you are the central character. So, it's time to look at *your* tender spots.

As we said, even if you have no intention of writing a memoir, you'll still find this useful: for poetry or fiction, or just to enrich your understanding of yourself and your life.

Think back to your childhood, to times when you felt alone. When you felt you had nobody to rely on but yourself. When you're ready to write, think about these questions:

- What judgments did you make about yourself?
  "That's the kind of person I am . . ."

- What judgments did you make about the world?
  "That's the way the world works . . ."

- What reflexes or default settings did this experience bake into you, for how you would deal with the world?
  "That's the kind of person I'm going to be, to get through life as easily as I can and protect myself from here on."

Set your timer  **and write**

When you're finished, read what you wrote aloud.

Write with Courage

Let's consider two kinds of courage: courage *about* your writing, and courage *in* your writing.

Maybe your ambition is to write something big: a sweeping science fiction trilogy, or an epic poem. You might feel embarrassed to share such a big ambition, especially if you're a beginning writer and you never received much encouragement. It's certainly smart to keep it under wraps around people who will tell you that you can't do it, you're not "special" enough, you're not "educated" enough. But if you keep your ambition completely hidden, it may start to feel like a fantasy rather than an achievable goal. Even if you don't feel sure you can pull it off, have the courage to share your ambition with people who will cheer you on. When you nail your colors to the mast, you make the ambition seem more possible to yourself—and at this point, your opinion about whether you can pull it off is the only one that matters.

Having courage *in* your writing is something different. Everyone has certain thoughts, or memories, or subject matter, that they shy away from. It's human nature to paper over ugliness, rationalize guilt, turn away from shame. But as a writer, this is some of your most powerful material—for the very reason that most people shy away from it. If there are areas in your life or your psyche that you find yourself avoiding when you write to these prompts, that's your imagination telling you it wants to explore your darker corners. If it didn't, the thought of writing about them wouldn't even occur to you.

We've urged you already to write without judging your writing. Now we're urging you to write without judging yourself. Does it upset you to think about something you once did? Have you had fantasies that scared you because they showed you what you might be capable of? You're not alone; even saints don't live unblemished lives. But how many people can write about their transgressions with honesty and insight? That takes courage.

The more you broaden your acceptance of your own human nature, the broader the range of your writing will be. Your own experience offers you the most vivid, heartfelt insights into the darker areas of our behavior spectrum as a species.

As you advance in your writing practice, you'll find the courage to write about your cruelties, betrayals, deceptions, and closely guarded secrets. Courageous writing is no-holds-barred truth-telling—to yourself. You don't have to share those truths. You can rip up the pages, or keep them under lock and key, or use the material for a fictional character. Nobody needs to know where you mined it.

If you're writing to these prompts in a group, you can pass instead of reading the piece aloud. But if you decide to share a dark piece you wrote, because you've come to appreciate the importance of reading your work aloud, you're showing a truly admirable level of courage. You probably feel like you're putting yourself on trial and you're afraid you'll be judged and found guilty, because what you're reading out is a confession.

In one workshop, a participant wrote about entertaining the possibility of murder as a way to solve a personal problem. When the 10 minutes ended, he reported that when the prompt was given, that particular experience popped into his mind and refused to let go. He had to write about it, whether he wanted to or not. He wrote about the fear of what he might have been capable of doing at the time, and his deep shame. The shame came back as he faced his fear of even writing about the incident. This was not, as he said, his official version of himself.

When we heard him read what he wrote, we judged him not as a terrible person but as a brave and committed writer. To his surprise, a number of people said that they too had once seriously contemplated murder—and they felt comforted by knowing they weren't alone. When you dare to explore and share your own darknesses, you give other people the courage to accept theirs.

Much of this writer's shame drained away, and, as a bonus, he realized that his imagination had given him a gift. As he wrote about turning away from murder, he remembered that he'd gone and bought an ice cream cone, and described the sensation of the sticky rivulets of melting ice cream snaking down his wrist—cold ice cream, instead of warm blood. You might think that "good writers" come up with powerful images such as that one by thinking, "I want an image here that will pack a punch." Most writers don't think this way. Like the turtle crossing the highway in Session 5, images like that are gifts of the imagination.

It takes courage and practice to let your imaginative mind take the lead. Your rational mind may resist, because it likes to stay in control. It's afraid of two things, chaos and madness. So it tends to shy away from material that might upend your view of the world or yourself, and it can panic if it thinks cherished certainties might get smashed. It takes courage to go to those edgy places. You can take comfort from the fact that you'll only be doing it for 10 minutes! The timer will ping and your short foray into scary territory will be over.

The goal of this training isn't to use writing therapeutically, but that's frequently a side effect. Writing this kind of material and sharing it lifts a burden from your psyche which you might have been carrying for a long time, and the people who read or listen to it may also feel a burden lifting from their psyches, thanks to you. When you hear your own voice reading your confession aloud, you find a new level of self-acceptance. And when other people reflect back to you their appreciation of your honesty and courage, rather than harsh moral judgment, your pendulum tips back to the "I'm an okay person" side.

Now, let's say that despite the value you've found in reading your work aloud, there is absolutely no way you will share your exploration of a secret you intend to take to the grave. If it holds this kind of charge for you, it's very powerful material. Give yourself the gift of using this material, by being courageous enough to explore it in the privacy of your notebook.

It's quite an achievement for a novelist to elicit sympathy for a true villain. Ever wonder how they do it?

"In the vaults of our hearts and brains, danger waits. All the chambers are not lovely, light and high. There are holes in the floor of the mind, like those in a medieval dungeon floor—the stinking oubliettes, named for forgetting, bottle-shaped cells in solid rock with the trapdoor in the top. Nothing escapes from them quietly to ease us. A quake, some betrayal by our safeguards, and sparks of memory fire the noxious gases—things trapped for years fly free, ready to explode in pain and drive us to dangerous behavior."

— Thomas Harris, *Hannibal*

Session 9:
There's No Story If Nothing Changes

Throughout the Writer Training, you've been exploring how human beings experience the world—which is the stuff of story. Now, we're moving from the imaginative storm to the creative form.

Change is a constant in life, and we tell stories to help us understand how life changes us. The question is, how do you pull a satisfying story out of the continuum? Where does a story begin and end? How does it take shape? What turns a sequence of events into a compelling story?

A vital part of the answer is to make character drive story. In the pieces you've written so far, you've seen how actions resulted from your loves and hates, hopes and fears, desires and decisions, emotions and judgments, and most of all tender spots. The rest of the answer depends on narrative structure. To approach this topic from an analytical perspective, check out the "Books We Recommend" section. Our goal here is to help you develop an intuitive sense of the most important components of story: beginning and ending, conflict and obstacles, turning points.

What do those story elements *feel* like?

Seed the Storm

Prompt: Sources of energy

Think about moments in your life when your emotions or your motivation got heightened. What gives you energy? Make a list.

Set your timer (2) and make your list now

Here are some sources of energy from other Imaginative Storm participants. Maybe you'll recognize some of these as true for you, too. Feel free to add them to your list.

frustration	*a deadline*	*receiving a compliment*
eye contact	*an epiphany*	*trees blowing in a storm*
laughter	*the desire to help*	*bodies in close contact*
rain	*dogs barking*	*ideas landing on me*

Now, choose one of the sources of energy on your list—something unexpected or very personal . . .

. . . and imagine if the entire world was powered by that source of energy.

Set your timer (5) and write now

When you're finished, read what you wrote aloud.

When you accepted the premise "What if," you began a story. As a result of that premise, things in the world you wrote about changed. Expectations were upended. Things may have seemed to go well at the start, but obstacles arose and, almost certainly, unexpected consequences ensued.

Story is all about things not going according to plan. If you go to Grandmother's house and she greets you with milk and cookies, you play a few rounds of cards with her, and then you go home, there's no story. But if you meet a wolf along the way and he's hungry, all kinds of things can happen.

Maybe you wrote about what might happen if the whole world was powered by coffee, or deadlines, or the desire to help. When you get a wild idea like this, grab hold of it and take it to an extreme. It's fun, it energizes your imagination—and often it sparks ideas and images you might want to use in your "real" writing. You can always dial it back later.

Prompt: Troublesome technology

Technology is supposed to help us. That's its sole reason for existing: to make something easier for humans to do. But often it doesn't.

In this prompt, you'll describe a person—yourself or someone you know or invent—who can't get to grips with a piece of technology. Technology is not necessarily advanced electronics or whizz-bang machinery. You can think of fire and language as technology—helping us survive, helping us communicate. The wheel is a classic example of technology.

Don't choose a smartphone! You can be more imaginative than

that. And feel free to stretch the definition of "technology." Here are a few intriguing examples from other participants:

- *sourdough baking*
- *a child getting used to shoes*
- *the discovery that Earth is round, not flat*
- *reusable shopping bags*

As you write, think about what it is in this person that makes them unable to do something that other people do easily. How do they deal with the frustration?

Set your timer (10) and write now

When you're finished, read what you wrote aloud.

That recalcitrant item of technology created an obstacle. The person you wrote about wanted to do something, but an obstacle stood in their way. You might think of the obstacle as the technology itself— or as the person's inability, or impatience, or refusal to learn.

Obstacles create story. If you're hungry and go to the fridge for a yogurt, big deal. If the fridge is empty, or there's no fridge because it's the tenth century, you'll have to go out and hunt for food. It might not come easily. What if there are no rabbits nearby? What if a wolf, or somebody you fancy from the tribe down the road, is hunting the same rabbit you're hunting? What if all you can find is an unappetizing, perhaps poisonous, bug?

The James List: Hard choices

Every move you make requires a choice. Some are easy, like wearing a coat in winter or clearing the table after a meal. Others are more challenging, like lending a friend money that you know they won't pay back, or defying your parents by going to art school instead of medical school (or vice versa).

What makes a choice hard? The stakes are high either way. Even if it turns out well, it comes with a cost. Hopefully you'll have gained more than it cost you, but who knows? Things may go wrong, or the risk may not have been worth it. When you make a hard choice, you never know for sure if you're doing the right thing. You just have to trust.

Think back to times in your life when you've been faced with a hard choice, and make a list.

Set your timer (5) **and make your list now**

Choices define character and drive story. Hard choices make a story intriguing. Which way will the character jump? What will happen as a result?

If you're writing fiction, devise hard-choice situations for your characters. If you're writing memoir, look for those moments of difficult choice in your life. They're turning points.

Prompt: The desire line

Stories happen because people make them happen. Somebody wants something and takes action to get it. And even if obstacles, like a wolf, stand in their way, their desire is strong enough to keep them going.

Look back at your James List. Desire drove those choices you made. There was a desire pulling you the other way, too—that's why it was a hard choice. But one desire won out over the other.

For this prompt, pick one of those hard choices to work with. You made this choice and took action because *you* wanted to do it. It was your idea, nobody else's. Maybe you ran away from home or ditched a well-laid plan. Maybe you chose to reject someone else's idea of you and took yourself back.

As you write, ask yourself these questions:

- What forced you to make that choice?
- What did you want, or need, or hope for?
- What held you back or stood in your way?
- What was at stake?
- What fears did you overcome?

When you're finished, read what you wrote aloud.

Asking the question "What does this character want?" is the fail-safe way to keep a story on track. When a character takes steps to get what they want, they expect a certain result—and if they get the expected result, story fades away. Story builds when they meet obstacles, they have to change their plans, and the stakes rise—meaning, things get riskier, the possible loss if things don't work out is greater. When your main character gets what they want, or their goal drifts forever out of reach, or they realize they didn't want it after all, your story is over.

The desire that drives a story can be huge, like defeating the source of evil in the universe. Or it can be very simple, as in the *Odyssey* and the many stories based on it, where the main character is just trying to get home.

Remember, it's not just your protagonist who has a desire line. Every character in your story wants something. So, think about what all your characters want. When two characters want opposing things, or both want the same thing but can't both have it, you have dramatic conflict. In the end, one will win—or they'll both lose.

Surf the Storm

Prompt: The disturbance of an equilibrium

An air conditioning unit crashes onto the sidewalk in front of you. That disturbs your equilibrium—though you could just walk around it, let the adrenaline subside, and get on with your life. But what if it hit the person in front of you? What do you do next?

The moment when an equilibrium is destroyed is a potential start for story, because it sends the people in the story on a quest to restore the balance. Humans are order-making creatures. When an equilibrium is destroyed, we search for a new one. And when we find it, we breathe easy. That's the end of a story.

But don't assume that you're supposed to start at the beginning when you sit down to work on a story. Like Barbara Kingsolver and many other excellent writers, you may not yet know where the beginning is. For example, Allegra's memoir, *Love Child*, is the story of a girl putting together the pieces of a fragmented family. You'd think it would have been blazingly obvious that the story begins when Allegra was told, at the age of four, that her mother had been killed in a car crash. But because there was material she wanted to include that took place chronologically before that day, it took her over a year of generating material before she realized that that was the moment when her equilibrium was destroyed and nothing could ever be the same again. Now, with the one parent she knew gone, she needed something: to know where she belonged.

Don't worry until later about where your final draft should start. Just generate material that you think belongs somewhere in the story; if it took place chronologically before the beginning you eventually decide on, you might include it as backstory, or a flashback, or a memory. But even if you don't use that material in your final draft, it served you in finding your beginning. No writing you do is wasted.

Fiction writers will often say that they're more likely to know where a story starts than where it ends. They often put characters in a situation and ask, "What if . . .?" Memoir writers are often inspired to write because they feel that a life experience has been completed in some way—so they're more likely to know the end of their story than the beginning. This is a pretty random observation which may help you, or it may not. Just take comfort in knowing that very few writers know both the beginning and end of their story when they start working on it.

As you go about your days, think about times when something suddenly changed the progress of your life. Maybe it turned your world upside down. Maybe you met someone and fell in love, or learned a stunning secret, or made one of those hard choices you wrote about. It might have been an event that didn't seem like much at the time, but looking back, you see that after that day, when Ryan didn't kiss Alex goodbye, nothing could ever be the same again.

You might like to make a list of such moments in your life, or the lives of people you know, to give yourself some ideas of what to write about. Don't worry about whether this incident could actually be the beginning of your story. For now, we just want to give you a sense of what a strong beginning *feels* like.

When you've settled on an incident, consider these questions:

- What could not continue?
- What expectations were upended?
- What was suddenly important or unimportant?
- What possibilities were closed off?
- What possibilities opened?
- What desire arose in you?
- What need arose in you?

Set your timer **10** **and write**

When you're finished, read what you wrote aloud.

We'd like to credit John Truby's book The Anatomy of Story *for the concept of the destroyed and restored equilibrium.*

Write in Safety

Creativity is not safe. You're creating something out of nothing and you never know if you'll be able to do it or if it will be "good enough." You're writing what you don't know, so you're on unsteady ground. You may be dealing with material that's genuinely horrifying or difficult. You may be exploring personal material that brings up loss, pain, anger, guilt, or shame. Nasty beasts and pitfalls lurk everywhere.

As a writer, you don't owe it to your readers to make them feel safe. In fact, maybe you owe them the opposite—a challenge, a shift of perspective, an expansion of their awareness. You don't have to create a new Hannibal Lecter. Eve Ensler shocked people, so did Kurt Cobain, so did Michelangelo and the Impressionist painters. But you also don't have to be a groundbreaking genius—just offer your readers something beyond the accepted collective fiction of the way things are or should be.

You need support when you venture into these multiple areas of unsafety. Perhaps your own confidence and commitment are enough. And if you're writing just for yourself, you aren't vulnerable to the slings and arrows of other people's responses. But if you do decide to put your work out in public, even just to a writing group, there are risks.

You hear a lot about a "safe space." The parameters are pretty simple. Openness to other points of view. Generous, committed listening. Appreciation, not criticism. And, in our opinion, writing prompts rather than sharing your "real" work.

Any situation where you have to put your big girl or big boy pants on and listen silently to the group's opinions about your work is not a safe space. In creative writing courses that use this model, the people criticizing you are, understandably, more interested in impressing the teacher and getting a good grade than in serving you. This is how the struggle sessions of the Chinese Cultural Revolution worked, as they "reeducated"—read, humiliated—the "bourgeoisie." But many people think they have to suffer this if they want to be serious writers. This is a cultural shibboleth which you do not have to buy into. You do not have to suffer to be a good writer!

If you plan to publish, you do want to see if your writing is having the effect on readers you want it to have. At this point, you don't want just praise and appreciation. You need to know if something's not working—if it's dull, or repetitive, or confusing, or not believable. Here, your practice of writing without attachment serves you again. If you're not attached to every word you write, you can accept other people's responses without defensiveness and see opportunities to make your work as good as it can possibly be.

Some people like to read their work-in-progress to a group, but that might not suit you. Your writing process may not be the same as other people's, and, whatever it is, if you are inspired and energized to keep working, your process is perfect. We believe that it's usually more helpful to get feedback on your writing one on one. That way you can engage your reader in a conversation that generates ideas and possibilities which go way beyond thumbs-up/thumbs-down.

Feedback should be given with one motivation only: to help you. Is that writer who offered to read your work competitive or opinionated? Say no thanks. A family member or close friend who might have unresolved issues with you, or be afraid to hurt you, or genuinely think everything you do is amazing? No thanks. Choose people who are your target audience—so, for example, if you're writing a complex sci-fi novel, don't give it to someone who only reads bodice-rippers (or vice versa). And find people for whom you can return the favor—because it is a big ask. It could be 10 hours, 15 hours, of somebody's time. That way, also, as you're taking turns in the hot seat, you'll both be motivated to be kind. Honest, but kind.

We've talked before about writing without judgment. Keep your own notebook a safe space. In your notebook, there is no such thing as bad writing—there's only writing and no writing. Its pages can contain anything. It can be a refuge or a high-wire act practice zone, or anything in between. Your rational mind knows that when you close it, any chaos and madness your imagination generated is held safely inside.

As you write more of what you don't know, writing playfully and with courage, without trying, without criticism or censorship or attachment, you are creating a natural bubble of safety around yourself. You're willing to let the process inform you. You trust that there will be something there, even if you don't always recognize what it is immediately—and if there isn't, on any particular day, that's okay too. If you find yourself in the doldrums of uncreativity, you know that the wind of inspiration will pick up again as soon as your curiosity is engaged. Keep writing what you don't know.

"If writing did not exist, what terrible depressions we should suffer from."

— Sei Shōnagon, *The Pillow Book*

Session 10:
The Oxymoronic Inversion

If you think back over the Writer Training, you'll notice how many pieces you wrote turned on contradictions, oppositions, and reversals. When you ranted—about something you hate that other people love, or something you love that other people hate—you reversed expectations. When you considered what wasn't there in a place, you may have noticed a contradiction between reality and how something was supposed to be. When you wrote about the elements, you collapsed the boundary between the natural and the artificial. When you investigated a "villain" character, you probably found a contradiction between the person's external and internal selves.

Your rational mind loves to assign categories to people, things, and experiences. But reality rarely falls into categories, as your rational mind wants it to do. Your imagination is amused by this. It gets fizzy and energized when you question the neat interpretations and judgments your rational mind has made. Like a dog gnawing happily on a bone, it latches onto contradictions that can't be explained away, oppositions that can't be resolved, and reversals that couldn't be expected.

What's the oxymoronic inversion? Just a phrase that came to us one day, and it stuck.

Seed the Storm

Prompt: How needy are you?

In Session 8, you explored what need might be at the heart of the trajectory of your life. Here, we'll widen the focus.

What do you need to live? What do you need to be sane? What do you need to be happy? Make a list.

Set your timer (2) and make your list now

Now, tick the five needs that are the most important to you. And then, as you write, consider these questions:

- Have those five needs all led you in the same direction?
- Or have you found yourself in a tug-of-war between them?

Set your timer (5) and write now

When you're finished, read what you wrote aloud.

Most people are contradictory in one way or another—which is what makes human nature so unpredictable and intriguing. In a funny way, recognizing your own contradictions makes you feel more human.

Prompt: Oppositions

The universe is patterned by dialogues of opposites—night and day, matter and antimatter, positive and negative electrical charges, and so on. Maybe that's why our minds gravitate toward these oppositions.

Begin by making a list of oppositions. Here are a few to get you started:

free/trapped   *frightening/comforting*
order/chaos   *beautiful/ugly*
up/down   *serious/ridiculous*
dark/light   *helpful/obstructive*

Add 10–20 more of your own.

Now, let your eyes roam over your list of oppositions until your imagination hooks onto one of them, and write about a time when that opposition defined a situation.

Set your timer (**10**) **and write now**

When you're finished, read what you wrote aloud.

Did the opposition you wrote about stay binary? Some oppositions become three-sided—for example, unhelpful is actually the opposite of helpful, but obstructive is worse. The opposite of order is disorder, but chaos takes things to a whole new level (except, maybe, if you're a chaos theorist and find order in chaos—there's an intriguing contradiction). If you're not free, you're trapped—but what if someone is keeping you prisoner? What if the person who betrays you is your best friend—and then they justify their betrayal by insisting they did it because they love you?

Sometimes the halfway point seems worse than the negative. For example, halfway between truth and lies is evasiveness. Have you ever dealt with someone being evasive and wished they'd just be straightforward and lie?

You can be so wrapped up in the extremes that you can miss the nuance in between. The black and white we see with our eyes are actually infinite shades of gray. Is there a night without a little starlight, or a day without shade? Could it be that the opposition between day and night is what makes dawn and dusk so precious?

You generate energy in your writing when you crash opposites and contradictions together. So keep asking your imagination to look for them: in events, in places, in people.

The James List: Shibboleths

What's a shibboleth? We'll define it as a saying that people commonly hold but which is often demonstrably untrue. They're a strong creator of personal and tribal identity, and their power overwhelms logic.

Here are some examples:

Artists have to suffer.
Love conquers all.
The body knows how to heal itself.
If you put gas into a car when the engine is running, it will explode.
What happens in Vegas stays in Vegas.

Now, make your own list of shibboleths.

Set your timer (5) **and write now**

Now, read your list of shibboleths aloud. Commit to each one, like you really believe it. Can you feel in your body when you're 100% on board with the shibboleth, and when you're not? Are you 100% on board with any of them?

What's so interesting about irrational beliefs like this is that the same person might buy into two that contradict each other. For example, you might know someone who believes both that if you "put it out there" you can manifest your desires and also that it's bad luck to talk about something before it happens. Maybe that person is you.

The human bias is to accept evidence if it supports what we want to believe, and discount anything that belies it. Even if there's some truth in shibboleths like these, they're not facts and they're not laws. The certainty they promise is an illusion. If you cheat on your spouse in Vegas, the secret may stay in Vegas but your marriage won't remain in its pre-Vegas state. The only thing that really stays in Vegas is your money.

You can use irreconcilable beliefs like these to reveal character and generate story. Face your character with situations where their cherished shibboleth leads them astray or just can't hold. How far will they go to uphold that belief, or defend it? People believe many things that don't stand up to reality, but they'll live by them, even die for them.

Prompt: The magnetic paradox

Life is always throwing us curve balls: things that turn out to be something very different from what you expected, things that end up meaning the opposite of what you think they'll mean in your life. Paradoxes like these are magnetic to both the rational mind and the imagination. Your rational mind longs to resolve them. Your imagination loves the ongoing discovery that they cannot be resolved.

See if your imagination hooks into one of these paradoxes:

- A paradise that was also a prison (it doesn't have to be a place; it could be a state of mind)
- A great burden that was also a deep joy
- A handicap that was a source of great strength
- A struggle that was also a comfort
- A catastrophe that brought you a treasure

If none of these grab you, think back to some time in your life that centered on a paradox like these.

Now think: what energy did that paradox generate?

Set your timer **10** **and write now**

When you're finished, read what you wrote aloud.

You might think it bizarre to become grateful for losing your mother at the age of four. But that was what happened to Allegra when she wrote her memoir, *Love Child*. She realized that if her mother had not died, she would not have had either of her two fathers, whom she loved very much.

Here's another example: when Navé was diagnosed with prostate cancer, he was devastated at the prospect of losing his sexual function. What he didn't expect was that his life would become filled with a deeper, richer sensuousness.

Many great stories have a paradox or a 180-degree reversal at their heart. What paradox or reversal might be at the heart of yours?

Surf the Storm

Prompt: One Last Lunch

For this prompt, you'll write a short story about something that's probably never occurred to you before. Allegra will tell you where it came from:

> One day, out of the blue, I received an email from a stranger named Erica Heller, asking me to contribute to an anthology titled *One Last Lunch: A Final Meal with Those Who Meant So Much to Us.* In the book, 49 people imagine what it would be like to have lunch with someone who is now dead. Erica wanted me to have lunch with my mother, who was killed in a car crash when I was four.
>
> Though I agreed to write the lunch, I was terrified of how emotionally grueling it might be. Finally, I built up my courage—and discovered that writing the lunch

brought me closer to my mother than I'd ever thought possible. There was a fantastic reversal at the heart of it, which I didn't realize until my mother sat down across from me: I was older than she was. My mother was 39 when she died, still caught up in the storms of romance and the desperate anxieties of parenthood. I was in my early 50s, and I'd weathered those storms. Having spent my whole life wishing my mother was alive to comfort me, I was able, over lunch, to comfort her.

Who would you choose to have a Last Lunch with? Where and when would the lunch take place? What would you eat? Would you be happy to see each other? What age would your loved one be? What age would you be?

Don't worry about trying to find a paradox or reversal before you sit down to your lunch. It will come as you write.

We won't ask you to set a timer for this one. Take as much time as you need.

If you'd like to hear Allegra read her Last Lunch, go to the Imaginative Storm channel on YouTube.

Write On

You now have a fat file of writing. It may seem disconnected: bits and pieces written to random prompts, with no obvious through-line. That's as it should be: when you're training, you're not deliberately sitting down to write a story or a memoir, just as a runner doesn't start training for a marathon by asking a friend to meet them 26 miles down the road.

In fact, this trove of writing that you've amassed may not be as disconnected as it seems. You could think of each piece as being like a sapling in an aspen grove. Did you know that an aspen grove in Utah is the largest single organism on the planet? A grove is actually all one "tree," with hundreds, maybe thousands, of trunks. They look like separate trees, but they're not; they're all connected beneath the surface as one single growing thing.

Some of the shoots and saplings in an aspen grove never get very far. Some can reach 80 feet—supported by the activity of all the others, as they draw nutrients from the dark recesses of the earth, the swirling patterns of water, and the dancing colors of sunlight.

The connections among the aspens are subterranean and invisible, but they are what give each individual "tree" its life force. The same is true of what you've written and what you will write.

Wander back through your aspen grove. Does that little shoot show promise? Is that one already starting to look like a tree? You might have the beginnings of a short story, or a novel, or a memoir, or a screenplay. You might have discovered that your natural form of expression is minimalist, compressed, elliptical—it tends toward poetry. You might already have a project in mind, such as a cookbook, and you can now see ways to make it more personal and engaging.

Consider typing up all this material, and highlighting phrases or ideas or insights that you want to develop. Revisit the prompts and generate more material—many of our prompts, such as "I don't re-member," can be used again and again. You might also enjoy writing to totally random prompts, such as you'll find on the Imaginative Storm YouTube channel and Instagram profile. Trust that whatever you write will connect up to your larger project in some way, even if the connection isn't obvious. It's all coming from the same genera-tive place, just like that aspen grove.

Ask yourself questions. As you did when you were a child, ask "why" and "why" and "why." Let your curiosity lead you into form.

Most of all, when you look back over your work, at whatever stage, be kind to yourself. Your inner critic should have a much better sense of how to be useful by now, so don't let it fall back into its old unhelpful ways. Allow it to identify passages that can be improved, but don't let it chastise you for not having written them better to begin with.

Above all, make sure you appreciate what's powerful and authentic, what's surprising and intriguing. That will give you the energy and the confidence to write on.

We'll leave you with one final prompt.

Think back over your experience of the Writer Training. Make a list of whatever words spring to mind.

Set your timer  **and make your list now**

Now, it's time to write. Consider this question:

What are the benefits of writing for you?

Set your timer  **and write now**

Write for longer if you like! And, as always, when you're finished, read what you wrote aloud.

Spread the Storm

If you teach writing, feel free to use this book. You can teach the entire Imaginative Storm Writer Training course in 10 or 11 sessions, or break it down further to cover a semester or even a school year. If you choose to use just a few of our prompts, please credit us.

If you're not teaching formally but would like to share the Imaginative Storm with your community, that's great! You can do this either by getting a group of friends to work through the Writer Training together, using this book or our online video course, or by starting an Imaginative Storm gathering.

An Imaginative Storm gathering is when a group of people get together, live or online, to write to a prompt. Here's how we do it:

We choose an image or an audio file to use as a prompt. Something strange. Something that holds many possibilities. We show the prompt for 2 minutes, and everyone generates a list of random words or short phrases. We then go around the circle and create a group list by asking everyone to contribute a word or short phrase from their own list. We then ask everyone to write for 10 minutes: whatever they want, long or short, prose or poetry, coherent or incoherent. Before we start writing, we remind everyone that this is a dance between the rational mind and the imaginative mind, with the imaginative mind leading the dance.

When the 10 minutes are up, we break into groups of 6–10 to

read what we wrote aloud. Then we all come back together and formally close the session at the top of the hour. After that, we usually continue on in an informal salon, discussing ideas and topics brought up by the members of the group.

You'll find an archive of all the prompts we've used in our online weekly gathering on the Imaginative Storm YouTube channel. Each video also contains our group list of words and some commentary from us on how it all fits together.

Our gathering is open to whoever wants to join us; you'll find the link at imaginativestorm.com. Many of the people who attend our gathering regularly say this writing practice has enriched their entire lives. It would make us very happy to know that you're doing this work and spreading the Imaginative Storm all over the world.

The key to a successful Imaginative Storm session, whether it's the Writer Training or a prompt gathering, is your willingness to take on the role of organizer and facilitator. Your friends will appreciate it! But keep in mind that you are also a member of the group, so it's important that you write and share your writing just like everybody else. That fosters a sense of equality.

And finally, if you're inspired either to use the Imaginative Storm method in teaching or to start your own gathering, please remember that it's vitally important to create a safe space. Honor everyone's privacy and authorial integrity. Everything shared in the gathering should stay in the gathering, unless the writer chooses to make it more public.

Lead by example:

- Praise and appreciate. Don't criticize.
- Don't play favorites or allow competitiveness to intrude.
- Be inclusive.
- Support and encourage everyone, so that everyone will support and encourage one another.

We'd be glad to give you further guidance about hosting an Imaginative Storm gathering, or help you create a lesson plan if you'd like to use the Imaginative Storm method in an academic setting. Please contact us through our website, imaginativestorm.com.

Books We Recommend

Jill Bolte Taylor. *My Stroke of Insight*. Viking, 2006.

Julia Cameron. *The Artist's Way*. TarcherPerigee, 2016.

Federico García Lorca. "Theory and Play of the Duende." Read on YouTube by A Poetry Channel.

Ross Gay. *The Book of Delights*. Coronet, 2020.

Elizabeth Gilbert. *Big Magic: Creative Living Beyond Fear*. Penguin, 2016.

Natalie Goldberg. *Writing Down the Bones: Freeing the Writer Within*. Shambhala, 2016.

Erica Heller, ed. *One Last Lunch: A Final Meal with Those Who Meant So Much to Us*. Abrams, 2020.

Allegra Huston. *How to Edit and Be Edited: and polish your work to a professional shine*. Twice 5 Miles, 2019.

Stephen King. *On Writing: A Memoir of the Craft*. Scribner, 2020.

Anne Lamott. *Bird by Bird: Some Instructions on Writing and Life*. Anchor, 1995.

Robert McKee. *Story: Substance, Structure, Style and the Principles of Screenwriting*. ReganBooks, 1997.

James Navé and Allegra Huston. *How to Read for an Audience: and touch people's hearts*. Twice 5 Miles, 2019.

John Frederick Nims. *Western Wind: An Introduction to Poetry*. McGraw-Hill, 2005.

Pat Schneider. *Writing Alone and with Others*. Oxford University Press, 2003.

John Truby. *The Anatomy of Story: 22 Steps to Becoming a Master Storyteller*. Farrar, Straus and Giroux, 2008.

And also, a terrific resource for writers:

KN Literary Arts. Coaching, editing, design, marketing. knliterary.com.

Acknowledgments

We'd like to thank everyone who has ever done a writing workshop with us. We learned a great deal from you, and your creativity and conversation enriched this book.

Special thanks to our beta testers for Imaginative Storm Writer Training: Stacey Christensen, James Coats, Adrienne Crew, Andrea Davis, Abdullah Erakat, T.L. Forsberg, Cameron Gregg, Kelly Hanson, Mary Hertert, Mona Khash, Jamil Mahuad, Poetic Prezz, Wendy Shaw, and Katerina Tana.

About the Authors

Allegra Huston and James Navé are co-founders of Imaginative Storm Writing Workshops and the publishing company Twice 5 Miles. They have been teaching multi-day and single-day writing workshops together and separately for over 20 years. For five years they taught a creativity retreat for screenwriting students at the National University of Ireland, Galway, and both have also taught for the University of Oklahoma OSLEP program.

For more details on their courses and workshops, visit:

imaginativestorm.com
Instagram: @imaginativestorm
Facebook: Imaginative Storm
LinkedIn: Imaginative Storm
Youtube: youtube.com/@imaginativestorm

James Navé is the author of two books: *The Road* and *100 Days: Poems After Cancer*. He was a co-founder of the legendary company Poetry Alive!, which sent teams of performance poets into schools across the U.S. to recite the classics to over 5 million students. He has taught poetry and creativity in schools on five continents. For six years he conducted Artist's Way Creativity Camps in partnership with Julia Cameron, author of the perennially bestselling guide to creativity *The Artist's Way*. He hosts a weekly podcast, *Twice 5 Miles Radio: Fertile Ground for Conversations Worth Listening to and Remembering*, which airs on WPVM-FM Asheville and KCEI-FM Taos.

jamesnave.com
Instagram: @jamesnave
Facebook: James Navé
LinkedIn: James Navé

Allegra Huston is the author of *Love Child: A Memoir of Family Lost and Found*, the novel *A Stolen Summer* (in hardback as *Say My Name*), *How to Edit and Be Edited,* and *How to Read for an Audience* (with James Navé), and a contributor to the anthology *One Last Lunch: A Final Meal with Those Who Meant So Much to Us* (edited by Erica Heller). She wrote and produced the award-winning short film *Good Luck, Mr. Gorski,* and has also written numerous feature screenplays. She has written for publications including French *Vogue; Condé Nast Traveler, Newsweek, Mothering,* and the *Santa Fean* in the US; and the *Oldie, Perspective, The Times, YOU* magazine of the *Mail on Sunday,* and the *Independent on Sunday* in the UK. She was Editorial Director of the UK publisher Weidenfeld & Nicolson for five years, and has worked as an editor for over three decades with authors including three Booker Prize winners, two Nobel Prize winners, and Jane Goodall.

allegrahuston.com
Instagram: @allegrahuston
Facebook: Allegra Huston
LinkedIn: Allegra Huston

If you enjoyed *Write What You Don't Know: 10 Steps to Writing with Confidence, Energy, and Flow,* please post a review on the site of your favorite online retailer.

About Twice 5 Miles

Twice 5 Miles publishes books, e-books, and courses designed to improve the quality of life for everyone who likes to learn.

Currently available in our series "Twice 5 Miles Guides—The stuff nobody teaches you":

How to Make a Speech: and inspire your audience, by Barrie Barton

How to Edit and Be Edited: and polish your work to a professional shine, by Allegra Huston

How to Read for an Audience: and touch people's hearts, by James Navé and Allegra Huston

Find these and future titles at twice5miles.com and online retailers, or order through your favorite bookstore.

www.ingramcontent.com/pod-product-compliance
Lightning Source LLC
Chambersburg PA
CBHW070709130626
46553CB00005B/1916